The Enduement of Power

The Enduement of Power

by

Oswald J. Smith, Litt.D.

Rickfords Hill Publishing Ltd.

RICKFORDS HILL PUBLISHING LTD.
Perch Cottage, Halton Lane, Wendover. HP22 6AZ.
www.rhpbooks.co.uk

First Published in 1933
This edition 2003
Reprinted 2008

ISBN: 978-1-905044-11-5

Typeset by Avocet Typeset, Chilton, Aylesbury,
Buckinghamshire.

Cover design and print production for the publisher by
Bookprint Creative Services, <www.bookprint.co.uk>
Printed in Great Britain.

Contents

WITH THY SPIRIT FILL ME

Oswald J. Smith   B. D. Ackley

1. Lord, pos-sess me now, I pray, Make me whol-ly Thine to-day;
2. Lord, I yield my-self to Thee, All I am or hope to be
3. Lord, com-mis-sion me, I pray! Souls are dy-ing ev-'ry day;

Glad-ly do I own Thy sway, With Thy spir-it fill me.
Now and thru e-ter-ni-ty, With Thy spir-it fill me.
Help me lead them in Thy way, With Thy spir-it fill me.

CHORUS

With Thy spir-it fill me, With Thy spir-it fill me;

Make me whol-ly Thine, I pray, With Thy spir-it fill me.

1

The Spirit-filled Life

Have you ever been filled with the Holy Spirit and are you living a Spirit-filled life today? The Bible says, "Be filled with the Spirit" (Eph. 5:18). Have you obeyed and are you filled?

This, you see, is a command – "Be filled with the Spirit." As a matter of fact, it is the most important commandment in the Bible. I know that the command to be baptized is important, but this is more important. The commandments of Moses are important, but they are not nearly as important as this commandment. The commandment of Jesus, "Go ye into all the world and preach the Gospel," is one of the most important in the New Testament, but the command to be filled with the Spirit is still more important. Because, you see, when you obey this commandment you automatically obey all the others. The fulness of the Spirit settles every problem in your life.

This commandment was not given to a carnal church; it was given to one of the most spiritual churches, the Church at Ephesus. If it had been given to the Corinthian Church we would have understood it at once. The Corinthians were carnal; they needed the fulness of the Spirit. But it was not given to them. If, therefore, it was necessary for the Ephesian Church it is necessary for us today. Paul could stand in any pulpit in our day and say, "Be filled with the Spirit," for there are some in every church who have never yet been filled with the fulness of the Spirit of God.

This message, therefore, is for each and every one of us. We all need to be filled with the Spirit. The disciples were filled on the day of Pentecost and then filled again at a later date. We, too, must be filled again and again. God wants us not only to be filled, but to live Spirit-filled lives. Otherwise we will be failures.

"But," you say, "I have the Holy Spirit. I received Him when I was regenerated." That is true. It was also true of the Ephesians. They had the Spirit. However, it is one thing to "have" the Spirit, it is another thing to be "filled" with the Spirit.

Here, for instance, is a glass of water. It is filled partly with water and partly with air. Before it can be filled with water all the air must be excluded. Only when it is filled to the brim would I be correct in saying that it is filled with water. So it is with you. You have the Spirit, but does He have you? Is He in complete control of you? Does He fill you? Or are you partly filled with the Spirit and partly filled with self, the world and sin? Does He dominate and rule your life? Are you really and truly filled with the Spirit?

When you are filled with the Spirit, you will be controlled by the Spirit.

Why Must You Be Filled?

But why must you be filled with the Spirit? There are two reasons and I express them both in one word, and that one word is POWER. You need power. You must have power. But power, however, along two lines.

First, Power Over Sin. You will never be an overcomer until you are Spirit filled. The Bible says: "Walk in the Spirit and ye shall not fulfil the lust of the flesh" (Gal. 5:16). It is only as you are filled with the Holy Spirit that you are able to overcome your besetting sin. The Holy Spirit makes you a victorious Christian. Without His fulness you will be defeated, you will be a slave to sin. God wants to set you free. He wants to make you an overcomer. You cannot overcome yourself. Only the Holy Spirit within you can overcome. The Christian life is the out-living of the indwelling Christ. Only as He indwells in the fulness and power of the Holy Spirit will your outward life be the kind of a life it should be. Therefore, in order to have power over sin you must be filled with the Spirit.

Second, Power in Service. You will never be used of God until you are filled with the Spirit. The Bible says: "Ye shall receive power, after that the Holy Ghost is come upon you: and ye shall be witnesses unto me" (Acts 1:8). If you are going to be an effective witness you must be filled with the Spirit. Otherwise you will witness in the energy of the flesh and accomplish nothing. If you want your testimony to count for God, you must testify in the power of the Holy Ghost. Only as you are filled with the Spirit will you be used of God, otherwise your ministry will be ineffective. You will be working in the energy of the flesh instead of in the power of the Spirit. Therefore, if you want God to use you, you will have to be filled with the Spirit.

This, then, is the purpose of the fulness of the Spirit, namely, *Power.* Power over sin and power in service. Do you have that power? Are you a victor? Are you an overcomer? Are you living a Spirit-filled life? Or are you a defeated Christian? Are you discouraged? Do you feel like giving up? Does your besetting sin still conquer you? Or have you been set free?

Then, too, do you have power in service? Is God using you for His glory? Are you really surrendered? Will you go where He wants you to go and do what He wants you to do? Are you His slave? Is He your Lord and Master? Is your testimony effective? When you witness for the Lord Jesus Christ does anything happen? Are you ministering in the energy of the flesh or in the power of the Spirit?

What Are the Conditions?

Now comes the question, "How may I be filled with the Holy Spirit?" What are the conditions? There are five steps that must be taken, five conditions that must be met. Let me express them in five simple words – confess, renounce, surrender, obey, believe.

1. *Confess*

In 1 John 1:9 we read: "If we confess our sins, He is faithful and just to forgive us our sins." Sin confessed is sin forgiven, and sin forgiven is sin cleansed. "The blood of Jesus Christ His Son cleanseth us from all sin" (1 John 1:7).

Note, if you will, that it is the Christian and not the sinner who is told to confess his sins. God never tells a sinner to confess his sins. First, because it would be impossible for him to remember them. He might remember some of the outstanding sins of his life, but there would be thousands that he would forget, and if he has to confess one then he has to confess all.

In the second place, if we were to tell a sinner to confess his sins we would be putting salvation on a basis of works, and salvation is not of works, but by faith. When a sinner wants to be saved you do not tell him to get down and start working by confessing his sins. You simply point him to the Lord Jesus Christ. All that a sinner has to confess is that he is a sinner and that he needs salvation. The Publican cried: "God be merciful to me, a sinner" (Luke 18:13). He did not confess his sins. He simply admitted that he was a sinner and needed mercy.

However, when it comes to the Christian it is entirely different. The Christian who has back-slidden and has gone off the road must return. Christian, in Bunyan's *Pilgrim's Progress*, tried to go on, but found that he had to return to the crossroads where he had slept, and there he found his scroll, and only then could he go on his way rejoicing. So it is with the Christian today. Some besetting sin in his life turned him aside and got him off the road. He must confess that sin before he can be right. God says: "If we (we Christians) confess our sins (the sins of the Christian) He is faithful and just to forgive us *our* sins" (again, the sins of the Christian). Anything that is wrong in the life of a Christian must be confessed. God will never pour out His Spirit on the flesh. Sin and spirituality cannot co-exist. The Holy Spirit will not occupy a dirty heart.

Now, let me ask you a question: Have you confessed every sin? Have you made everything right between you and those you have injured or wronged? If you have borrowed money, have you paid it back? Or are you still in debt? God says: "Owe no man anything" (Rom. 13:8). Have you paid what you owe, or are you refusing to meet your obligations? Where do you stand with your fellow men? Where do you stand with God? Have you come clean? Do you believe God has forgiven you?

2. Renounce

Not only must you confess your sin, you must also renounce it. It must be put away. Unless you forsake what you are doing, your confession is valueless. It is no use confessing your sin and then going right back and committing it again. When sin is confessed it must also be renounced. "If I regard iniquity in my heart, the Lord will not hear me" (Ps. 66:18).

But, you say, I cannot give up my sin. I am a slave to it. I love it. It has a strangle-hold on me and I cannot break it. My friend, let me ask you two questions. First, are you *willing* to forsake your sin? Second, are you *determined* to forsake your sin?

Now there are a lot of Christians who are not willing. They turn it over as a sweet morsel and they do not want to give it up. Do you remember when Jesus spoke to the man at the pool? He said: "Wilt thou be made whole? Do you want to be better, or would you rather be sick?" If, my friend, you are not willing, then you will have to offer this prayer: "Lord, I am willing to be made willing," and God will make you willing.

You may be willing and yet not be determined. The Prodigal Son was willing. He was sick of the life he was living. He wanted to get away from the swine, but he was not determined. Finally, however, there came a moment when determination took the place of willingness. Springing to his feet, he cried: "I will arise and go." Turning his back on the swine, he started towards his father's house, and never looked over his shoulder until he found himself in his father's arms. As soon as he was determined he was free. You, too, must be determined. You must be dead in earnest. You must mean business. If you are both willing and determined, God will set you free.

3. *Surrender*

Up to the present we have been dealing with the negative, now we turn to the positive. It is one thing to confess and renounce, it is another thing to surrender. The Bible says, "Yield yourselves to God" (Rom. 6:13). God wants you to serve Him and in order to serve Him you must be surrendered to Him. Everything must be laid on the altar. You are His, body, soul and spirit. Not only is He your Saviour, He is your Lord and Master.

The reason you have had so much trouble in your Christian life is because your will has crossed God's will. There will never be an end to the struggle until your will parallels God's will. His will must become yours, so that you can say with the Lord Jesus in the Messianic Psalms, "I delight to do Thy will, O my God" (Ps. 40:8). "My meat is to do the will of Him that sent me" (John 4:34). Once God's will has become your will the conflict is over. After that you will have no desire to do anything apart from the will of God. You will have surrendered completely to the Lord Jesus Christ.

The trouble with most of us is we have never been broken. We have never really yielded. Let me show you what I mean.

Sam Jones, the well-known American Evangelist, held a campaign for the cowboys of Texas. They wanted to take up a love-offering for him, but they had no money, so they let him go back to his home in Philadelphia without any honorarium. Some weeks later he received a telegram from the cowboys stating that they were sending him a love offering. They were shipping him a carload of bronchos. But what could Sam Jones do in the city of Philadelphia with a carload of wild horses? Suddenly he thought of an idea. He decided to hold an auction sale and sell them and then pocket the money, which he did.

However, he kept the finest-looking animal for his son. Calling the cowboy to him, he asked him the question: "How much will you charge to break this broncho so that my son can ride him?" "Fifteen dollars," said the cowboy. "Take him away," said Sam, "and break him." Two weeks passed by. The cowboy returned, leading the broncho. "Is he broken?" asked Sam. "Yes, sir." "Can my son ride him?" "Yes, sir." "All right, here's your fifteen dollars."

Then Sam, thinking that he had better try first, approached the animal. The cowboy came running up in consternation. "Why, what's the matter?" asked Sam. "Why, sir," said the cowboy, "he has only been broken on one side and you are mounting from the wrong side." "Oh," said Sam, "that will never do. My son might make a mistake and mount him from the wrong side. How much will you charge to break him on the other side?" "Fifteen dollars," said the cowboy. "All right," said Sam. "Take him away and break him on the other side."

Another two weeks passed and the cowboy returned with the broncho. "Is he broken now?" asked Sam. "Yes," said the cowboy. "Both sides?" "Yes, sir, both sides. Your son may mount from either side." "All right," said Sam, "here is your fifteen dollars. "

Do you know the trouble with the average Christian? He is only broken on one side. He is like Ephraim's cake – half-baked. He will do this, but he will not do that. He will go here, but he will not go there. He will sing in the choir – if he can sing the solos. He will work in the foreign field, but he refuses to work in the home field. God cannot depend upon him. He has never been broken. He still wants his own way. He is not trustworthy. God wants us to be broken, so that He can count on us. Once that has happened we will be surrendered and then we will be usable. If God were to fill us with the Holy Spirit and we still chose our will instead of His, we would make shipwreck of the experience. We must be broken, yielded, surrendered, if we are to be filled.

I will never forget the time God broke me. It was when I was quite young in the ministry. I had been pastor of a large Presbyterian church, but I had resigned. Naturally, I expected to get another just as large, but I found that I could not. I preached for a Call in many a church, but was never called. I went to small churches, much smaller, even to mission halls, but still I was not wanted. My finances were very low and I was at my wits' end.

One day Paul Rader came to Toronto to hold a great campaign in Massey Hall. I asked if I could usher and I did so, but was soon set aside. Then I tried to do personal work. But, again, I was ignored. Finally, I started selling hymn-books in the aisles.

My heart was broken. I knew not which way to turn. It seemed as though my ministry had come to an end and that I was to be put on the shelf. I felt that God had no more use for me. I was desperate.

Suddenly, one night, Arthur W. McKee, Paul Rader's song-leader, announced that he was going to lead the great congregation in the singing of a new hymn that had just been published, entitled "Saved". Then before the entire audience of 3,400 people he pointed down to where I was selling hymnbooks and said: "That young man down there wrote this hymn." I did not know which way to look. I went on selling hymn-books.

Presently the audience began to sing. I will never forget it. I was hearing it for the first time. I was to hear it often in the after years.

But as I went home that night God spoke to me. There came into my heart a conviction that I was not going to be laid aside, but that I was going to be used again. And so it came to pass. The great Alliance Tabernacle was built and the world-famous Peoples Church founded.

Suddenly one day I received a cable from London, England, asking if I could occupy the world-famous pulpit of Spurgeon's Tabernacle for a few Sundays. I immediately accepted. For years now I have never been without a Call. I have to refuse dozens that I cannot accept. Before long I was travelling all over the world holding large campaigns.

But, you see, I had to be broken. God knew that I was proud and ambitious, and so He could not use me. He had to bring me down by taking everything away from me, and only when I had completely surrendered, only when I had been broken, was He able to trust me again and use me for His Glory.

4. *Obey*

God says that He gives the Holy Spirit "to them that obey Him" (Acts 5:32). Obedience follows surrender. If you are truly surrendered you will obey. You will endeavour to do God's will at all times. God will not fill a disobedient Christian. As soldiers must obey the commands of their officers so you must obey your Lord and Master, Jesus Christ. Are you an obedient Christian? If you are God will fill you with the Holy Spirit.

5. *Believe*

Have you taken these four steps? Have you confessed, renounced, surrendered and obeyed? If you have, then all you have to do is to believe. God will then give you a supernatural faith and you will be able to trust Him for the fulness of the Holy Spirit. Remember, the Holy Spirit is more anxious to fill you than you are to be filled. Nature abhors a vacuum. So it is with the Holy Ghost. As soon as your heart is ready He will come in and then He will complete the transformation until you are finally changed into Christ-likeness.

What Will Be the Evidence?

There may not be any great emotional experience. God never promises it. No two are filled the same. When there is a lot of sin there may be a tremendous experience. When there is a big dam and it is suddenly taken away, there will be a mighty rush and roar as the water pours over. If there is no great dam, then, as you quietly yield, He will flow in in His fulness and fill you without any tremendous upheaval, but it will be real nevertheless.

The result will be seen in your ministry. You will be used by God. Conviction will grip the hearts of those to whom you preach, or witness. God will work in you and through you for His glory. He will use you as you have never been used before. You will then know both power over sin and power in service, and that will be the evidence of the Spirit's fulness, namely the fulfilment of the purpose.

Will You Do It?

Will you, right now, take these five steps? Will you get alone with God, and as you pour out your heart in confession, will you tell Him that you renounce every sin? Then will you yield to Him, surrender to Him, become His slave? Then obey. Do what He wants you to do. After that it will be easy for you to trust Him, to believe Him for the fulness of the Spirit, and you will rise to live for Him and serve Him in a way you have never known before.

There will be a peace you will experience for the

very first time, a rest you have never known. And, as you walk softly in fellowship with Jesus Christ, you will be conscious of His presence. You will know that He has filled you with His Spirit. Your problems will be solved, for you will have carried out the injunction given in Ephesians 5:18 – "Be filled with the Spirit."

2

The Promise of the Spirit

Pentecost was the birthday of the Church. For the first time the Holy Spirit, the third person of the Trinity, came to abide. Again and again during the closing days of His earthly ministry Christ had promised the Comforter. Hence it was expedient, He explained, that He go away, that the Paraclete[1] might come. Pentecost was the fulfilment of His promise, when from the Father's right hand He poured upon the waiting Church the Holy Spirit. He Himself had gone but He had not left them orphans. Through all their earthly pilgrimage, in the midst of fire and sword, the blessed Paraclete was to dwell within, sustaining and comforting until His own return.

Before I speak about the *fulness* and *anointing* of the Holy Spirit in relation to the believer, let me go back to the time before He was given and take a brief survey of the *promise* and its fulfilment; for His coming was foretold by John the Baptist, confirmed by Jesus Christ and fulfilled in the experience of the disciples.

---

[1]*Paraclete* is taken from a word used in the Greek original for the Holy Spirit, meaning 'intercessor, comforter'.

The promise by John is stated in Matthew 3:11, "I indeed baptize you with water unto repentance: but He that cometh after me is mightier than I, whose shoes I am not worthy to bear; He shall baptize you with the Holy Ghost and with fire."

The definite confirmation of this promise by Jesus Christ, in addition to the many times He spoke about the Holy Spirit in His final talks during His passion week, is stated in John 7:37–39 and Acts 1:4, 5. These passages read as follows: "In the last day, that great day of the feast, Jesus stood and cried, saying, If any man thirst, let him come unto me, and drink. He that believeth on me, as the Scripture hath said, out of his belly shall flow rivers of living water. (But this spake He of the Spirit, which they that believe on Him should receive: for the Holy Ghost was not yet given: because that Jesus was not yet glorified.)" "And, being assembled together with them, commanded them that they should not depart from Jerusalem, but wait for the promise of the Father, which, saith He, ye have heard of Me. For John truly baptized with water: but ye shall be baptized with the Holy Ghost not many days hence."

The fulfilment in the experience of the disciples is given in Acts 2:1–4, "And when the day of Pentecost was fully come, they were all with one accord in one place. And suddenly there came a sound from heaven, as of a rushing mighty wind, and it filled all the house where they were sitting. And there appeared unto them cloven tongues, like as of fire, and it sat upon each of them. And they were all filled with the Holy Ghost."

Now let us get the significance of all this. Imagine John baptizing in Jordan, and in connection with the baptism promising a second baptism to be administered by Another. That announcement would be a most startling fact. I can think of those who had been baptized recalling again and again the words of John and saying to themselves: "I wonder when that greater baptism by the Mightier One which John promised will take place?" Then at last, one day, they heard the promise confirmed from the lips of Jesus Himself. Twice over at least and possibly many more times was the confirmation given. Finally the day of days dawned. Pentecost had come. They were all in the Upper Room, when, suddenly, the promise which had been given by John and confirmed by Jesus, was gloriously fulfilled in their experience. The Mightier One had baptized them with the greater baptism.

Then followed the Pentecost of the Samaritans as given in Acts 8 where through apostolic mediation the Holy Ghost was bestowed.

But as yet the Gentiles had been barred. God must somehow break down the wall and let the Jews know in an unmistakable way that the Gentiles were also to become members of Christ's Body, the Church. And so Peter is sent to the household of Cornelius, though it necessitates a special vision to persuade him to offer the Gospel to those outside Israel. Then to the amazement of all, God gives to the Gentiles their Pentecost as well and does it in such an open and startling manner that Peter is utterly silenced. The glorious promise made by John and confirmed by Jesus has now been completely fulfilled in the experience of the disciples, Jews, Samaritans and Gentiles; and the Church where there is neither male nor female, bond or free, Jew or Gentile, has at last been fully launched.

3

The Fulness of the Spirit

The Bible distinguishes between "having" the Holy Spirit, which is true of all believers, and being "filled" with the Spirit, which is true of very few.

In John 3:3–8, we have regeneration by the Holy Spirit, and since the New Birth is an inward work, it is clear that the Holy Spirit enters in order to impart Life. Then in 1 Corinthians 3:16, we have these words: "Know ye not that ye are the temple of God and that the Spirit of God dwelleth in you?" From this verse it is clear that God's Spirit has taken up His abode in the Church, the collective body of believers. And in 1 Corinthians 6:19, it is evident that each individual believer has become a sanctuary of His indwelling presence, "Know ye not that your body is the temple of the Holy Ghost which is in you?"

Now let us turn to Romans, chapter 8, verses 9–16, and as we read, note specially that the word "Spirit", meaning the third Person of the Trinity, is usually spelt with a capital "S". "But ye are not in the flesh, but in the Spirit, if so be that the Spirit of God dwell in you. Now if any man have not the Spirit of Christ, he is none of His."

Now it is not necessary to spend much time on the

second statement, viz., that very few have been *filled* with the Spirit. Paul, in writing to the Ephesians, commanded them to "be filled with the Spirit" (Eph. 5:18). Paul did not give unnecessary commands. There must have been some who were not filled in order to bring forth such an injunction. And it is only necessary to observe modern Christians in almost any community to realize that all are not filled with the Spirit.

It simply means that there is a difference between the believer "having" the Holy Spirit and being "filled" with the Spirit.

And let me say that it is not a question of our getting more of the Holy Spirit, but rather of the Holy Spirit getting more of us. We allow Him to occupy one or two of the rooms, but we do not hand over every key and give Him access to every part. He must possess all for He is not the guest but the Head of the home.

There is nothing we need so much for our churches and homes, nothing so important for our missionaries and Christian workers, nothing that will count so much in our service for Christ, as the fulness of the Holy Spirit. In fact, God will hold us responsible for the souls we might have won, the work we might have accomplished, had we lived Spirit-filled lives.

God's Plan

God's plan is that every one should live a Spirit-filled life from the very moment of conversion, but practically no one does. Perhaps it is lack of teaching. I do not know. There seems to be a seventh chapter of Romans in every life. It is not God's will that any child of His should ever backslide. Nevertheless there are many backsliders. Hence, when they return to the Lord there is a second definite crisis in their lives. Thank God for the provision, the possibility of restoration. But oh, that they had never wandered away!

That is why I say that if people are not taught about the Spirit-filled life and led into it immediately after conversion, but are allowed to wander away, there will consequently be a second great crisis experience whenever it is revealed to them and accepted.

Hence, if you did not receive Him in His fulness at conversion, if there have been years of sin and failure, if you realize now that you are working in the energy of the flesh and not in the fulness of the Spirit, then it is your privilege to meet the conditions and experience His indwelling.

Such was the sad record of Israel. For forty years they wandered in the wilderness, though they could have gone straight through to the promised land in eleven days. Hence the experience of crossing the Jordan came nearly half a century after the first great crisis when they crossed the Red Sea. The wilderness with all its defeat and failure was left behind and the promised land entered, where victory and rest took the place of discouragement, murmuring, failure and defeat.

It was so with Jacob. In his vision of the ladder his

life was given to God. Many years later, however, on that never-to-be-forgotten night when there wrestled with him an angel of the Lord, he made a complete and full surrender, said an eternal "yes", and was wholly yielded to God. There was nothing to hinder him from walking with God from the night he saw the ladder vision, but he yielded to self for so many years after, that the great crisis did not come until his return journey.

If your life has been a life like Jacob's, useless to God and disappointing to yourself, if you have not gone right through from the beginning and lived wholly for your Lord, if you are still unsatisfied, let me tell you that you may come now, meet the conditions and know the fulness of the Spirit. It was definite in the experience of the Israelites. Never would they forget the crossing of the Jordan. A pile of stones in the bed of the river and another on the bank proclaimed to future generations the great national crisis. In the morning they were on one side, at night on the other. During the day, that one never-to-be-forgotten day, they had crossed clean over.

Leave then the old life and enter the new. You should have done it at conversion. It ought to have happened long ago. God did not intend you to wander for years out of His will. But, praise His name, He is ready even now to fill you the moment you meet the conditions. The Spirit has been given. He will not keep you waiting if you are ready. The fulness of the Spirit is the normal Christian life that God intended you should live.

The fulness of the Spirit will answer all your questions and settle all your problems about worldly amusements. Never again will you have to ask, "Is it right to go here? Is it wrong to go there? May I attend the theatre? What harm is there in the dance? May I play cards?" You will be so filled with Him that you will not want the world. It will be the expulsive power of a new affection. The new will expel the old. You will find your greatest delight in God's service, and you will discover that you are miserable and unhappy in the world.

God's Three Men

There are three representative men spoken of in the Bible. They are known as the natural man, the carnal man, and the spiritual man.

THE NATURAL MAN

The natural man is described in 1 Corinthians 2:14, where Paul says, "The natural man receiveth not the things of the Spirit of God: for they are foolishness unto him, neither can he know them, because they are spiritually discerned." The natural man is the unregenerate man; he has never been born of the Holy Ghost. He lives in the natural realm and is a million miles away from the spiritual. He can no more comprehend spiritual things than can the unborn child the world into which it has yet to come. Before he can know anything about the spiritual world he must be born into it. The two spheres are far apart. He knows many things within the circle in which he dwells, the natural; but outside that circle he is an utter stranger. He must be translated from the natural to the spiritual, and then only will he be able to comprehend things spiritual. It is for this reason that everything of a spiritual nature seems utter foolishness to an unsaved man or woman.

Here is an African. He has never seen ice. You tell him that in your country the water sometimes gets so hard and strong that you are able to walk on it. In fact, men, you say, drive teams of horses over it, drawing great sleighs loaded with logs. "Absurd," he replies. "Utter nonsense! I have lived in Africa for fifty years now. Water I have seen almost daily. Yet never once have I known it to be so hard that I could walk on it." Hence you give up in despair. Convince him you cannot. But you bring him home with you, and one morning the thermometer registers forty below zero. Now you take him out to a near-by lake, and he is convinced in a moment.

You tell me that fire burns, and then you try to give me an idea of what it feels like to be burnt, and I endeavour to understand. But my imagination fails me utterly. I have no conception whatever of the actual experience of a burn. But one day I touch a hot stove, and immediately I know what it is like. You do not need to explain any further. I know. I have felt it.

Thus it is with the natural man. To understand the things of the Spirit is impossible. Keen though he may be intellectually, brilliant and trained in mind, mighty in brain power – when it comes to Spiritual things he is like a little child. He has never yet experienced what he seeks to apprehend. The Biblical direction is, "Oh, taste and see." But he has never tasted; he has never seen. Hence he does not know.

To understand why you prefer a prayer-meeting to a theatre, or a Gospel Service to a dance, is utterly impossible. You see, he has no appetite for the things of God; hence he does not relish God's menu. It is not a question of intellectual apprehension, it is a question of appetite. To enjoy the menu of God he must have his appetite changed. After that he will enjoy nothing so much as a feast on God's Word. His new appetite will only be satisfied when he is feeding on the things of the Spirit.

That was why Philip said to Nathaniel, "Come and see." To argue would have been but a waste of time, for Nathaniel was a thinker. Philip knew that and so he answered Nathaniel's question by simply saying, "Come and see." Nathaniel, Philip knew, must meet Jesus for himself. And so must every natural man. There must be a personal experience.

THE CARNAL MAN

The carnal man is described in 1 Corinthians 3:1–4, where Paul declares, "I, brethren, could not speak unto you as unto spiritual, but as unto carnal, even as unto babes in Christ." The carnal man, therefore, is still a babe. Now everybody admires a baby, but if it remains a babe when it ought to be a man, it becomes an object of contempt. A baby is expected to grow up. And if a Christian remains a babe, there is something radically wrong.

Paul continues in the second verse, "I have fed you with milk, and not with meat: for hitherto ye were not able to bear it, neither yet now are ye able." Babies have to be fed. They have never learned how to take care of themselves. The Bible to them is a closed book, unless they can find someone to explain it. Their dependence is upon others for spiritual food.

"For ye are yet carnal: for whereas there is among you envying, and strife, and divisions, are ye not carnal, and walk as men? For while one saith, I am of Paul; and another, I am of Apollos, are ye not carnal?" The marks, therefore, of a carnal Christian are envy, strife and division. These too, are the marks of a carnal church.

It matters not how wonderful your testimony may sound, if there is envy in your heart, if you are at strife with your neighbour, if you are not on speaking terms with someone against whom you cherish a grudge, if you refuse to shake hands, forgive and forget, if your life is marked by division, you are not spiritual; you are carnal. For these are the signs of carnality. And I care not how spiritual a Church may profess to be, nor how seemingly successful its work, if its membership is divided so that there is strife and envy, resulting in split after split, that Church is carnal, not spiritual.

In Romans 8:7, Paul declares that "the carnal mind is enmity against God: for it is not subject to the law of God, neither indeed can be." An enemy it is and always will be, and the man who bows to it, yields to it, compromises with it, is counselling with a traitor in the camp. No Christian can afford to give place to it, or to have any dealing with it whatsoever.

There are two crimes in English law for which the death sentence is inflicted. One is murder and the other treason. Now, as I have said, carnality is a traitor, and the only thing to do with a traitor is to take him out and execute him. To allow him to live is to endanger the whole camp, for sooner or later he will bring disaster. See to it then that the old traitor, carnality, is taken out and executed. Make sure he is on the cross, dead and buried, and that there is no resurrection. Say with Paul, "I am crucified with Christ." Know that "Ye are dead". For, "our old man is crucified with Him". Be certain that it is an accomplished fact in your experience.

THE SPIRITUAL MAN

The spiritual man is mentioned in 1 Corinthians 2:15. Paul says, "He that is spiritual judgeth all things." In other words the spiritual man discerns. He is able to detect false doctrine and false fire. It matters not how much truth may be intermixed, if there is error he knows it. And oh, how we need this discernment in these days of apostasy and fanaticism! How busy Satan is, giving counterfeit experiences and gifts! How easy it is to be deceived. There is so much of the flesh in our meetings, so much that is not of the Holy Ghost, so much that is spurious, that if ever we needed a spirit of discernment, we need it today. The spiritual man is not always able to meet and combat error, but he can recognize and avoid it. He can warn others and thus protect the flock from the wolves who go about in sheep's clothing. Then in Galatians 6:1, Paul makes this statement: "Brethren, if a man be overtaken in a fault, ye which are spiritual, restore such a one in the spirit of meekness; considering thyself lest thou also be tempted." When a carnal Christian attempts to adjust differences between Christian brethren, or to deal with the sin of another, the result is often times disastrous.

Here, for instance, is a man who has fallen into sin. Immediately some carnal Christian hastens to the rescue. But, approaching in a spirit of superiority, a "holier than thou" attitude, filled as he is with self-confidence and spiritual pride, condemning the one who has fallen, he discovers that all his efforts are unavailing, and that the brother whom he seeks to win grows harder and harder every day and gets farther and farther away. Now send one who is spiritual, and what happens? Why, the brother is restored at once. The spiritual man goes first of all to the privacy of his own room, where he gets alone with God to seek the heart preparation that must be his before he even sees the one who has fallen. "Oh, Lord," he prays, "give me a broken heart, a contrite spirit, a real love for my brother. How easily I might have fallen had I the same temptations! What if I were now in his place!

And it might have been." Thus he remembers the warning of God's Word: "Considering thyself lest thou also be tempted." Now he is ready. With melted, broken heart he goes, humbly and lowly, and putting his arm around the one who has sinned, he breaks down and weeps. There are no words of condemnation, no accusations. He points to a God of mercy and tender compassion; the Holy Spirit works, and soon all is well.

These, then, are the three representative men of the Bible, the natural, the carnal, and the spiritual. Which are you? Are you living in Egypt, the world, and the home of the natural man, or in the wilderness, the abode of the carnal? Or have you been truly regenerated? Have you crossed the Red Sea? Are you already through the wilderness, over the Jordan, and dwelling in Canaan, the land of the spiritual?

The Purpose of the Spirit's Fulness

The purpose of the Spirit's fulness is for the bestowal of power. "Tarry ye in the city until ye be endued with power from on high" (Luke 24:49). "Ye shall receive power, after that the Holy Ghost is come upon you" (Acts 1:8). But power along two lines.

1. POWER OVER SIN

The natural man is void of the Holy Spirit. He is convicted from without by the Spirit, but until he is born again, the Holy Spirit does not enter to abide.

The carnal man has the Holy Spirit, but is in a continuous warfare because of the dominion and power of the flesh. This battle is described in Galatians 5:17, where it is stated that, "the flesh lusteth against the Spirit and the Spirit against the flesh: and these are contrary the one to the other: so that ye cannot do the things that ye would." Hence the flesh is often victorious and the Spirit defeated.

Soon after conversion the believer becomes conscious of this great battle raging within, the conflict between the flesh and the Spirit, the old nature and the new, each seeking to gain the mastery. And, to his dismay, he discovers that the old frequently dominates; in spite of himself he yields to the flesh. He loses his temper at times, impure thoughts lodge themselves in his mind, and other sins such as worry, anxiety, jealousy, pride, envy, malice, spite, unforgiveness, hatred, discouragement, despondency, irritation, discontentment, selfishness, greed, passion, lust, worldliness, and a host of unhallowed uprisings, clamour for recognition.

Against these he struggles, weeps and prays, but all in vain. At last, when he has tasted every experience in the unequal combat as described in Romans 7, he cries out in dismay: "O wretched man that I am! who shall deliver me?" It is then that he realizes the need of a power outside himself; and finally he makes the discovery that God has made full provision for just such an experience through the Holy Spirit who now undertakes and becomes, Himself, Master of the situation.

If you read carefully you will discover that in Romans 7:14–24 Paul is describing his own experience under the law, when he really wanted to serve God and tried his very best, exerted all his will power, but miserably failed. Hence, this passage describes the religious man of today, either saved or unsaved, who has never learned the secret of deliverance through Another, and who, therefore, endeavours to keep the law and serve God by his own efforts, but absolutely fails in spite of his vows and resolutions to be good. In verse twenty-four Paul, at last, admits his utter failure. In verse twenty-five he confesses that deliverance is to come through Christ. In chapter eight he explains that Christ's Agent for the accomplishment of this deliverance is the Holy Spirit. Paul now ceases his struggling and hands the battle over to the stronger One, the Holy Ghost. He himself, in spite of his will power, has gone down in defeat, unable to combat the law of sin within. But in Romans 8:2, he says, "The law of the Spirit of Life in Christ Jesus has made me free from the law of sin and death." Hallelujah! Now, "the righteousness of the law" (demanded by the law) is "fulfilled in us" (not by us, but in us) by the Holy Spirit as we walk and yield to Him (verse 4). Up to the end of the seventh chapter, the Holy Spirit practically never comes on the scene. In chapter eight, however, He is mentioned nearly a score of times. No longer can sin "reign within" (6:12). The great Emancipator has undertaken, and victory is assured. Praise God!

Look now at Ezekiel 36:27, "I will put My Spirit

within you, and cause you to walk in My statutes." Ah! now we have the secret. There is One already within who is to take control and do the work. The believer must recognize Him; must yield to Him. That is what Paul failed to do in Romans seven. He tried to do it himself. That is what he did do in Romans eight. "Walk in the Spirit and ye shall not fulfil the lust of the flesh" (Gal. 5:16).

Thus the carnal man now becomes a spiritual man. He is dominated, controlled and guided by the Holy Spirit. Victory over sin is his at last. And oh, the joy of victory through Another! Self-effort unavailing; struggles, vows and resolutions useless; "but God", God the Holy Spirit, equal to all emergencies – Glory to His name! With the spiritual man the desire for the old life is gone. He no longer hungers after the things of the world. Romans eight is now his experience.

The trouble with the carnal man is that he lives too near the enemy's territory. His only hope is to put the wilderness between himself and Egypt, and thus get so far away from the old life that he no longer hankers after the leeks and garlic of Egypt.

The carnal man always travels in a circle. Consequently he is today on the Egypt border, and tomorrow on the Canaan side. No wonder, then, that he looks with longing across the Red Sea, and occasionally when no one is watching makes a short excursion into Egypt. And, likewise, as he nears the Jordan in some great spiritual Convention, he experiences desires for a closer walk with God. Satan can use carnal Christians. The only real trouble in any church comes from uncrucified flesh. The spiritual is God's goal for every child of His.

2. POWER IN SERVICE

The carnal man can never be used in spiritual service. There is so much of the self life about him that God cannot gain control. The Spirit-filled life is necessary for fruitful Christian service. No country would ever dream of sending its soldiers to fight without proper equipment. Now the fulness of the Spirit is the Christian warrior's equipment for service. Apart from a Spirit-filled life he is helpless. With the Holy Ghost he is all powerful in God.

"Ye shall receive power, after that the Holy Ghost is come upon you: and ye shall be witnesses unto Me" (Acts 1:8). We need power to witness. Otherwise our testimony will be unfruitful. "My speech and my preaching was not with enticing words of man's wisdom, but in demonstration of the Spirit and of power" (1 Cor. 2:4). Thus Paul ministered. "They were all filled with the Holy Ghost, and they spake the Word of God with boldness. Now when they saw the boldness of Peter and John, and perceived that they were unlearned and ignorant men, they marvelled" (Acts 4:31, 13). Thus the apostles carried on their ministry, bore testimony and witnessed, preached and taught. God can accomplish more through one message in the fulness of the Spirit than through hundreds given in the energy of the flesh.

We need the Holy Spirit for prayer. "Likewise the

Spirit also helpeth our infirmities: for we know not what we should pray for as we ought: but the Spirit Himself maketh intercession for us with groanings which cannot be uttered" (Rom. 8:26). "Praying with all prayer and supplication in the Spirit" (Eph. 6:18).

There are some Christians who feel that they cannot pray in public. That would not be true if they were Spirit-filled. "The Spirit helpeth our infirmities." Spirit-filled Christians can pray and testify aloud. Well do I remember a woman in Dale Presbyterian church, Toronto, Canada, who could not open her mouth in prayer in public. One day I called on a Christian sitting behind her to lead in prayer "What if he had called on me?" this woman asked herself. But one night in the meeting this Presbyterian who had never, and could never, open her lips in public, began to pray in the Spirit with such liberty and freedom that every one was blessed and edified, and that spirit of prayer remained on her in mighty power for months after. "Where the Spirit of the Lord is there is liberty." If you have no liberty in prayer and testimony it is because you have not experienced the fulness of the Holy Ghost.

No man can really pray without the Holy Spirit. No one can experience true travail in prayer apart from the Spirit. Fleshly travail avails nothing. Spirit travail accomplishes the impossible and effects its object. To pray in the Spirit is to gain access to the throne of God. Do we really pray, then, or do we merely say prayers? Is there a spirit of travail that travails until it prevails? Without the fulness of the Spirit we will never know the true meaning of intercessory, travailing prayer.

What Are the Conditions?

What is the *secret* of a Spirit-filled life? Are there conditions to be met? There are, but they are only two in number.

FIRST, SURRENDER

"Yield yourselves unto God" (Rom. 6:13). Tell Him all about your failures, the vows you have made, the resolutions you have broken, the experiences of the wilderness journey, and with contrite heart hand your poor, broken, defeated life over to Him. Let Him take control. Ask Him to occupy the throne of your heart. Make a complete surrender, with full confession and renunciation of all known sin. That is the first step. Oh how much depends upon this! Discipleship is the real secret. To fail here is to fail everywhere. If your life is not Spirit-filled it is an evidence that you are not wholly yielded, surrendered, consecrated, obedient; for He fills what you yield.

But not only am I thinking of the surrender of self – of that I will speak later – for first of all there must be the surrender of sin. To surrender something simply means to give up that something. And sin, no matter how much I love it, must be surrendered.

The dearest idol I have known
   Whate'er that idol be:
Help me to tear it from Thy Throne
   And worship only Thee.

There must be a cleavage, a separation, a renunciation, a definite turning from and forsaking of all iniquity. The will, regenerated, can and must be dead set once for all against sin. If I really, truly, deep down in my heart, want to break with sin, thank God, I can, or rather, He can. Ample provision has been made. What, then, about that besetting sin? Have you surrendered it? Are you prepared to deny yourself the passing pleasure it affords? Again and again you have been deceived. When Satan held it out to you it looked like a bouquet of roses, but when you grasped it you discovered that it was filled with thorns. And oh, how they pierced you! What pain you endured! Surrender them. They are not worth the sorrow they leave.

Well, what about it? No trifling now. Have you confessed and put out of your life every sin? "Your iniquities have separated between you and your God, and your sins have hid His face from you, that He will not hear" (Isa. 59:2). "If I regard iniquity in my heart the Lord will not hear me" (Psalm 66:18). Sin must be confessed, renounced and forsaken. Otherwise God will not even hear the prayer offered. If wrong has been committed it must be made right. It may be that restitution will have to be made, and forgiveness sought from someone who has been injured. There can be no compromise with sin. Let alone answer the petition, God has declared that He will not even "hear", listen to the prayer. Then of what use to ask Him for the fulness of the Spirit if He will not even listen to the request?

Right here lies the crux of the whole matter. Men and women seek God in prayer, pleading for the fulness of the Spirit, spending long hours on their knees, and yet getting nowhere, simply because there is sin in the heart, and they will not pay the price. Unforgiveness, hatred, envy, or some other fleshly power holds sway. Every time they pray the Spirit of God reminds them of a wrong that has never been put right, and they attempt to hush His voice. But it is of no use. Sooner or later the sin question must be honestly faced and dealt with. It may be an unknown sin, for, "The heart is deceitful above all things and desperately wicked." Then there must come the cry: "Search me, O God, and see if there be any wicked way in me." And sometimes God has to take us down in the very dust, and give us a glimpse of our own hearts, until we cry out in horror at the sight as did Isaiah, Job and Peter, and confess the sinfulness of our very nature.

Am I ready now to part with iniquity? Can I say farewell to even my besetting sin? Do I want God's fulness enough to give up all I know to be wrong? Or, do I love my sin and am I unwilling to say "No" when temptation comes? These are the vital questions that must now be faced, questions that will determine whether or not I really want to live a Spirit-filled life.

Here, for instance, is a young woman who longs

to be Spirit-filled. She bows at the altar and pleads with God, but all in vain. Her heart is unsatisfied, and she gets nowhere. She wants to be filled, oh yes, but there is something in the way. At last she bares her very soul as she confesses that there is an obstacle, a hindrance, just one. She is interested in a young man who is not a Christian. He goes to church but will not yield to the Lord Jesus Christ. God has no hold on his affections and thus their paths divide. She remembers the uncompromising command of God: "Be ye not unequally yoked together with unbelievers," and she knows that God gives the Holy Spirit only to those who obey Him. Thus it resolves itself into a question of who comes first, God – or her unsaved companion. She struggles, weeps and pleads, but will not yield. Hence she cannot be filled. She has not surrendered.

Here is a young man who indulges in secret sin. No one knows anything about it, no one but God. Again and again he has vowed to give it up. Resolutions innumerable have been made and as quickly broken. Every time he sins he is filled with remorse, and there and then he promises God that if He will forgive him this time he will never fail again. And for a time he keeps his word, but the flesh is weak, and when the awful temptation comes again, once more he yields in spite of himself. Thus the Spirit's fulness is kept out because sin still reigns. He has not yet come to an end of himself, nor is he really willing to renounce and utterly forsake his besetting sin. When he is, the Holy Ghost will very quickly supply the enabling power. But first there must come his decision, his real attitude toward his sin. Then God will fill him with the Holy Spirit.

Somehow we get a false impression of our Father God. We think of Him as unwilling to bestow His Gifts. And, like the heathen, we plead and pray, groan and weep, urge and entreat, as we tarry at the altar, trying to persuade Him to give something that He is far more willing to give than we are to receive. We are so often like the prophets of Baal who cut themselves and cried aloud, but all in vain.

"How much more will your Father give the Holy Spirit to them that ask Him!" Oh, then, let us believe that God loves to give, that it delights His Father heart. He longs and yearns to bless. That is His nature.

I often think of the Holy Spirit as a mighty river, but a river dammed and held back by obstacles of one kind and another. Fancy a man standing on the dam and pleading in prayer with the river to flow on. How absurd! "Why," the river would answer, "that is just what I want to do. Don't waste your energy in such vain repetitions. It is my nature to flow. I'm more anxious to flow than you are to see me flow."

Ah, yes, that's the secret. There's a dam in your life, a dam of sin. There are obstacles in the way, obstacles of unyieldedness. You deal with sin. Do you hear me – sin! Get the bed of the river cleared and the river will flow all right. You will not even have to ask the Holy Spirit to fill you. In fact, you will not be able to keep Him out. He will come and fill of His own accord. Oh, how eager He is to enter!

How anxious He is to get control! Why not give Him a chance?

How will He come? Will there be any evidence of His presence, any unusual manifestation? Well, how does the river flow? If the dam is broken down suddenly the mighty river will roar and rush in one huge volume through the fresh opening. But when it comes to the slight depressions on either side farther down, it is merely a question of lifting the obstacle, however small, out of the way, and the water of the river, without a sound, will quietly flow in and fill up the space. Both are equally full, the deep bed and the slight depression. One was conscious of a great commotion, the other scarcely realized just when the river flowed in. Now if you have been allowing a great dam of unconfessed and unforgiven sin to enter your life, obviously when you take the dam away the change will be so great that you will feel as though you had suddenly been deluged. But with most Christians who are hungry for the Spirit's fulness it is a question of little obstacles, and as soon as these are all removed, everything that offends or grieves God, the Holy Spirit quietly enters and takes possession. It is enough to know that I am right with God, that all obstacles have been removed, for then I know, feeling or no feeling, that the river of the Holy Ghost flows through my life.

Suppose I were to call at your house, knock on the door and wait for you to let me in – what would you do? Would you fall on your knees in the hallway and beg me to enter? Would you plead with me to come in? Well, suppose you did, what difference would it make? How would it help matters? There I am on the outside, waiting, and oh, so eager to enter. There you are on the inside pleading and praying for me to come in. But there is the door between us, locked and bolted. What chance have I? How can I enter with such an obstacle in the way? You say, "Oh, Dr. Smith, please come in." And I say, "Open the door and I will gladly come in." "But, Dr. Smith," you continue, "I do want you to enter. Oh, if you could only know how I long for you to come in! I beseech you to come into my house." And thus with tears and sobs you pray and plead. And I answer as before, "Just open the door; it is in the way. Remove it, and I will come. I long to enter. I am eager to get inside. But the door is shut. You must open it." At last you stop praying and weeping. You arise to your feet, open the door, and I immediately step inside.

Oh, beloved, do you not see it? Is it not clear now? "How much more shall your Father give the Holy Spirit to them that ask Him?" Will you not believe me when I tell you that He, the Holy Spirit, is right at the door, eager, oh, so eager, to enter? And will you not be sensible and instead of weeping and praying, pleading and beseeching – will you not just open the door, remove the obstacles, confess and renounce the sin, and thus let Him in? Would I still hesitate if the door were open? Would you have to ask me the second time? Why certainly not. The moment you open the door that bars me out, I enter. Is the Holy Spirit more unwilling than I am? Why of course not! The fact is, He longs, He yearns to enter your heart and fill you. It is the door, the obstacle that hinders. Deal with that and all will be well. He will come in at once.

But did not Jesus command us to "wait for the promise"? Does He not say, "tarry until"? Yes, but that was before Pentecost. God's appointed time for the sending of the Spirit was the day of Pentecost. It was, "when the day of Pentecost was fully come". The disciples were certainly ready, but the Spirit had never been given. After Pentecost there was no waiting. Mark that – no waiting. Cornelius and his household did not tarry for ten days. They received at once even before they began seeking. The Samaritan Christians knew nothing of tarrying. They received as rapidly as Peter and John prayed. Paul's converts at Ephesus did not wait. Paul laid his hands on them and at once the Spirit was given. And so it always has been ever since the day of Pentecost. True, we oftentimes have to tarry to get right with God, but that is because we are so slow to confess our sins and accept His will. But on God's side there is never any waiting or delay.

To truly "tarry" or "wait" for the Spirit as commanded by Jesus, it would be necessary for us to go to Jerusalem, for He said: "Tarry ye in the city of *Jerusalem*" (Luke 24:49). But it is no more necessary now to still "wait" at Jerusalem for the Holy Spirit than it is to "tarry" at Bethlehem for Jesus. It was necessary before He came, for Bethlehem was the appointed place. Now He has come; He is here. We have but to "receive" Him. So, too, the Holy

Spirit has come; He is now here. We are to "receive" Him, to "be filled". And to still "tarry at Jerusalem" is to deny the fact that He came, as stated, on the day of Pentecost.

So, then, it is merely a question of real surrender, abandonment to God. Just as nature abhors a vacuum, and just as the air rushes in the moment there is an opening, so the blessed Holy Spirit, more anxious to fill the vacancy than the air we breathe, will fill your heart and life the very moment the surrender is truly made. The whole question therefore is one of surrender. Lay bare the obstacle, confess, renounce and forsake the sin, yield fully to God, and He will fill. Not only get right, but keep right. Every Christian knows exactly what it is that grieves the Holy Ghost and displeases God. Deal then with that thing, that Achan, whatever it is, and blessing will come. Walk with God and all will be well.

But how are we to continue filled? Why, just the way we began. Keep the obstacles out. Forbid the rebuilding of the dam. Walk in the light. So live that daily, weekly confession, for the same failure will not be necessary. Remember that "God giveth the Holy Spirit to them that obey Him". Then be obedient. Walk so that there will be no condemnation. In Galatians 5:16 you will find the needed guidance at this point. "Walk in the Spirit and ye shall not fulfil the lust of the flesh," How simple! "Walk in the Spirit", live in the Spirit, dwell in the Spirit, act, think and talk in the Spirit, and no longer will you be guilty of fleshly lusts. In other words, stay in

Canaan. Never emigrate to another country. Keep off the devil's territory. "Walk in the Spirit." Thus the Holy Ghost, unhindered, lives and moves in the life utterly abandoned to God. Feeling or no feeling, as long as we walk in the light there is no condemnation.

SECOND, FAITH

You are not to struggle, plead and wait. You are to take. You may feel no different; there may be no manifestation, or evidence, apart from the Word of God, but after all, what surer foundation can you have? God is faithful. If you have done your part, if you have truly surrendered, then believe that He accepts your surrender and fills you with the Holy Spirit, and go forth reckoning on that fact. I am not speaking now of the great mighty anointings such as were received by Wesley, Finney, Moody and others, a fresh enduement for each new service, sought and received as you wait before Him in fasting and fervent prayer; but simply of the secret of victory and blessing as a result of the Holy Spirit's indwelling and abiding presence, who does for you what you have failed to do, and who manifests Himself from the moment of conversion according to the measure that you recognize and yield to Him – the normal Christian life that God intended you should live.

"Be filled with the Spirit" (Eph. 5:18). Why this command? Because God wants you to be filled. You are not to get more of the Holy Ghost; He is to get more, yea, all, of you. No longer are you to use Him; He is to use you.

> *Once I sought to use Him,*
> *Now He uses me.*

He is to fill you that there may be no place for sin to operate. He is to reign that sin may not reign. Thus He becomes "the expulsive power of a new affection". Put your finger, then, on Ephesians 5:18, and believe God. What He demands is possible.

There is a great misunderstanding these days about "feeling" and "faith". It is so hard to get people to simply believe that God does fill them with His Spirit. They wait for feeling. Some special manifestation or emotional experience; some unusual demonstration must be theirs before they are Spirit-filled, they think.

Now I have made this very important discovery; viz., that when a Christian is weak spiritually, a new convert for instance, God does give feelings and manifestations, and that frequently: but when the believer becomes strong spiritually these ecstatic experiences and emotional manifestations are largely withdrawn. Now why? Simply because God's plan is that we should walk by faith and not by sight. The weakling must of necessity walk by sight, but the mature believer by faith. For instance, if I were to suddenly grab for the pulpit and lean hard on it, you would at once conclude that I had taken a weak spell and was ready to faint. Hence, I need support. I have to feel something and so I hold on to the pulpit. Now I have plenty of feeling in both my hands and against my body as well. But that is because I am weak. For as long as I am strong and well I never think of support. I stand erect on my own legs, feeling nothing, but perfectly normal. A little child learning to walk clutches the furniture because its legs are weak; but as it becomes mature it never thinks of props and supports at all. It is strong physically.

Beloved, if you are always looking for feeling, it is a sign that you are weak in the faith, for when you become strong spiritually, you will be satisfied to simply believe God, to rest upon His Word, regardless of your feelings. The thing that brings joy to His heart is to have His children walk by faith rather than by sight.

I remember one time I boarded a boat at Vancouver to go to Victoria. Making my way to a seat I sat down and surveyed the passengers. Now I felt quite all right. I had no fear, no doubt, no uncertainty. Had I not purchased my ticket, and was I not bound for Victoria? Why then worry? So far as my feelings were concerned I was on my way to Victoria and would be there in a very few hours. And so I gave myself up to the passing pleasures of the trip. Finally the purser came along to take up my ticket, and in a moment my feelings underwent a tremendous change. I had boarded the wrong steamer, so he told me, and instead of going to Victoria, I was bound for Seattle, Washington. But what was it that made the difference? My feelings? Oh, no! My feelings failed me entirely so far as guidance was concerned. It was the purser's word. Not until he had spoken did I know my situation, and as a result of his word, my feelings immediately underwent a change. It was his word, you see. And so, dear one, if you for a moment depend on your feelings, you, too, may be deceived. You must get something better than feeling under your feet.

Your only safety therefore is God's Word. It never, never, never changes. What He has written, He has written. "The Scripture cannot be broken" (John 10:35). And whether it be for salvation or the fulness of the Spirit it is all the same. So find out His terms, His conditions; meet them, and the result promised is yours. Whether you feel different or not has nothing to do with it. You are different because He says so. If John 1:12 tells me that I become His child by receiving Jesus Christ, then I know I am His child because I have received Christ. And all the feelings in the world will never alter His Word. If He tell me that I am Spirit-filled when my life is yielded wholly to Him, when I walk in the light, and do only the things that please Him – when I become obedient; then I know that I am Spirit-filled because I have and I do meet His conditions. There is but one question I have to ask, and it is this: Am I right with God?

Thus, beloved, we walk by faith and not by sight. Oh that we might become mature believers, and seek no more the feelings of an emotional experience, but dare to believe God, taking our stand once and for all on His promises. The devil can counterfeit many an experience, but he has no substitute for

God's Word. "It is written," defeats him every time. I care not if I go for months without any special feeling; if I am walking with God, if I am living in the centre of Hs Will, then I know that His Spirit indwells and I am satisfied.

> *Once it was the blessing,*
> *Now it is the Lord;*
> *Once it was the feeling,*
> *Now it is His Word.*

Do you remember that wonderful day when Peter, James and John were with Jesus on the mountain top? And do you recall just what actually transpired? You think, of course, of the light above the brightness of the sun, and of Moses and Elijah who appeared there with Jesus, and of the strange suggestion made by Peter, the spokesman of the group. Let us listen to him:

"Master," he exclaims, "isn't this marvellous! Why, I never had such an experience in my life before. What a light! How bright it is! Oh, I feel just wonderful! Let us build three houses here, Master. I want to stay and enjoy this glorious experience all the rest of my life."

Do you wonder at him? Why, there never was such feeling and manifestation, such a remarkable demonstration as that. It was truly a mountain-top experience.

But presently the light fades, Moses and Elijah disappear, and looking up they see no man save Jesus only.

"Come on," says Jesus. "Come along, Peter. This is all right for a few moments, but this is not what we are here for. There is work to do, Peter. Other sheep I have. The perishing multitudes must be reached. My Message is for all the world. Just at the foot of this mountain is a father with a demon-possessed boy. Come along, Peter; we must work the works of Him that sent us while it is day; the night cometh when no man can work." And down they go.

The light has faded, the experience passed, the feeling gone, but – He, Jesus Himself, is with them still. Oh, hallelujah! "Lo, I am with you alway, even unto the end of the age. I will never leave thee nor forsake thee. As I was with Moses so I will be with thee." And that is better than the best experience after all. "Did not our heart burn within us, while He talked with us by the way?" Ah, dear one, seek no more the feeling; be content to toil on and on with Him, doing what He bade you do, remembering that He is with you and will be even unto the end.

> I'd rather walk with God in the dark
> Than go alone in the light;
> I'd rather walk by faith with Him,
> Than go alone by sight.

But, you ask, will there be no feeling? Oh, yes! At most unexpected moments, when you are not even thinking about it. God will not forget you. Many a time He will shower blessing upon you. Not because you seek it, not because you ask it, nor because you tarry for some special demonstration, but because you believe God, because you do His will, because you are walking by faith and not by sight. And feeling, as a rule, comes in service. It is your business to get the Gospel out, and as you do it, like the disciples of the Early Church, you will be filled with joy and with the Holy Ghost.

What is the Evidence?

What is the *evidence* of the Spirit's fulness? How are we to know when we have been filled? Is there any result that can make us certain? Most assuredly there is. And if you have been following closely what I have said about the purpose of the fulness, then you will agree with me at once when I state that the evidence is the fulfilment of the purpose; namely, power over sin and power in service.

What was the evidence to Elisha that he had received a double portion of Elijah's spirit? Was it some ecstatic feeling, some special manifestation? It was not. The evidence was that Elisha now had Elijah's power, so that when he, too, smote the waters of the Jordan with Elijah's mantle, they divided as they had for Elijah. The evidence comes in service.

Now, of course, there are many other results: great peace and heart rest, exaltation of spirit, joy unspeakable and full of glory, a new realization of the presence of God, freedom and liberty in testimony and prayer, an inexpressible longing for God, and satisfaction in Him alone; a new and blessed separation from the world, and a spiritual love before unknown.

In one way or another the Holy Spirit will manifest Himself, but never to all alike, for He divides "to every man severally as He will". Great floods of joy, feelings like waves of electricity have been the experience of some, but not all. If ever a man was filled with the Holy Spirit that man was Chas. G. Finney. Now Finney did not receive the gift of tongues. But he did receive power for service. Conviction settled down upon those with whom he came in contact, revivals broke out everywhere, and thousands were saved.

The great question is: Have I power, power over sin, and power in service? If I have, then I am living the Spirit-filled life, and if not, then I do not know this experience. It matters not what my gifts may be, what success I attain, or what spiritual manifestation I have. Unless I have power over sin, and power in service, I am not living in the fulness of the Spirit. This and this alone is the evidence.

4

The Anointing of the Spirit

It is an undeniable fact that all down the centuries God has anointed men with the Holy Ghost. Even in the Old Testament dispensation this divine equipment was given as well as in the New. Again and again it is said of Samson that "the Spirit of the Lord came upon him". Saul and David were likewise anointed. The prophets had the same experience. Space forbids the mention of scores of prophets, priests and kings, whom God definitely endued with power from on high for the special work He wanted done.

The same record is borne in the New Testament. The Spirit of God resting upon the heralds of the cross enabled them to do what no man could accomplish of himself. Peter and Paul preached in demonstration of the Spirit and of power and thus the Early Church grew by leaps and bounds.

The past nineteen hundred years furnish abundant evidence of this power in the lives of men. Missionaries of the cross have gone to the darkest lands and accomplished the impossible because of the anointing resting upon them. Evangelists have wrought until multitudes have been swept into the Kingdom, and revivalists, endued with power from on high, have transformed whole nations. Such were the mighty leaders of early Methodism and the first workers in the Salvation Army. In fact individuals could be cited in almost every branch of the Christian Church who have known the mighty anointing of the Holy Spirit. Such has been the experience of all great spiritual leaders, as I have already shown in my message on "Power from on High."[1] Those who have read the biographies of John Wesley, Chas. G. Finney, D. L. Moody, and hundreds of others of all denominations, will recall that nearly every one testifies to having experienced a mighty anointing of the Holy Spirit. The fact that different men have expressed this experience by the use of various terms does not lessen the strength of their testimony. The great thing to keep in mind is the fact that after they had been saved, sometimes long after, something happened that revolutionized their lives.

Go back, if you will, into the history of any denomination and you will discover this to be true. Numerous cases might easily be cited among Presbyterians, Methodists, Baptists, Congregationalists, Anglicans, Moravians, Mennonites, as well as in the Salvation Army and many other smaller sects and denominations. We have on record the testimonies of men in all branches of the Christian church, and the universal experience has been a great crisis known as conversion, followed by a second definite experience, in which the life has been wholly yielded to God, filled with His Spirit and a new

---

[1]*The Passion For Souls.*

power received never known before. Hence we are not emphasizing something abnormal or unique, since every outstanding Christian leader all down the centuries bears witness to what has been stated.

Therefore, to refuse to believe in such an experience is to deliberately reject the testimonies, not only of the reliable witnesses whom we have quoted, but also of an innumerable host that might be cited from every denomination and sect of the Christian church, all of whom claim to have been anointed with the Holy Spirit, though they used different words to express it.

Take, for instance, the testimonies of D. L. Moody, Chas. G. Finney, and Wm. Bramwell, men whose word cannot be doubted. And for the sake of greater emphasis we will let them speak for themselves.

D. L. Moody

"The blessing came upon me suddenly like a flash of lightning. For months I had been hungering and thirsting for power in service. I had come to that point where I think I would have died if I had not got it. I remember I was walking the streets of New York. I had no more heart in the business I was about than if I had not been in the world at all. Well, one day – oh, what a day! I cannot describe it, I seldom refer to it; it is almost too sacred an experience to name – right there on the streets the power of God seemed to come upon me so wonderfully I had to ask God to stay His hand. I was filled with a sense of God's goodness, and I felt as though I could take the whole world to my heart. I took the old sermons I had preached before without any power, it was the same old truth, but there was new power. Many were impressed and converted. This happened years after I was converted myself. I would not now be placed back where I was before that blessed experience if you should give me all the world – it would be as the small dust in the balance."

Charles G. Finney

"As I turned and was about to take a seat by the fire, I received a mighty Baptism of the Holy Spirit. Without any expectation of it, without ever having the thought that there was any such thing for me, without any recollection that I had ever heard the thing mentioned by any person in the world, the Holy Spirit descended upon me in a manner that seemed to go through me body and soul. I could feel the impression, like a wave of electricity going through and through me. Indeed it seemed to come in waves and waves of liquid love; for I could not express it in any other way. It seemed like the very breath of God. I can recollect distinctly that it seemed to fan me, like immense wings.

"No words can express the wonderful love that was shed abroad in my heart. I wept aloud with joy and love; and I do not know, but I should say I literally bellowed out the unutterable gushings of my heart. These waves came over me one after the other, until I recollect I cried out, 'I shall die if these waves continue to pass over me.' I said, 'Lord, I cannot bear any more'; yet I had no fear of death.

"When I awoke in the morning instantly the Baptism I had received the night before returned upon me in the same manner. I arose upon my knees in bed and wept aloud for joy, and remained for some time too much overwhelmed with the Baptism of the Spirit to do anything but pour out my soul to God."

William Bramwell

"When in the house of a friend at Liverpool, whither I had gone to settle some temporal affairs, previously to my going out to travel, while I was sitting, as it might be, on this chair [pointing to his chair], with my mind engaged in various meditations concerning my present affairs and future prospects, my heart now and then lifted up to God, but not particularly about this blessing, *heaven came down to earth;* it came to my soul. The Lord, for whom I had waited, came suddenly to the temple of my heart; and I had an immediate evidence that this was the blessing I had for some time been seeking. My soul was then all wonder, love and praise."

*

Oh, my brethren, have we the anointing? Are we preaching "in demonstration of the Spirit and of power"? Does the unction rest upon us? Is there a freshness to our testimony? Are people convicted, saved and edified under our ministry? Or are we living in a past experience?

The question is: What new anointing did I receive last week? Is my experience up-to-date? So many testify to something wonderful that occurred years ago, but their lives are so barren and dry that it is clear they long ago lost the freshness of what they received. We should be anointed again and again, a fresh anointing for each new service.

The Importance of the Anointing

God considers the anointing of the Holy Spirit of paramount importance. In Luke 24:49, Jesus commanded His disciples to "tarry until endued with power from on high". And in Acts 1:4 He "commanded them that they should not depart from Jerusalem, but wait for the promise of the Father, which, saith He, ye have heard of me. For John truly baptized with water: but ye shall be baptized with the Holy Ghost not many days hence". Nor was there the slightest thought of attempting to minister without this power. And just think: all the world was in darkness; none knew the Story; they alone had been entrusted with the Gospel; men were perishing on every side; yet they were forbidden to make a move until anointed with the Holy Spirit. How important, therefore, Jesus considered it!

We read in Acts 10:38, "How God anointed Jesus of Nazareth with the Holy Ghost and with power: who went about doing good, and healing all that were oppressed of the devil: for God was with Him." And in Luke's Gospel we have the actual historic fact of this incident recorded. Let us quote first from Luke 3:22: "And the Holy Ghost descended in a bodily shape like a dove upon Him, and a voice came from heaven, which said, Thou art my beloved Son; in Thee I am well pleased." Here Jesus Himself is anointed with the Holy Spirit. Now let us note the result. Look at the first verse of the fourth chapter. It reads as follows: "And Jesus, being full of the Holy Ghost, returned from Jordan." Next at the fourteenth and fifteenth verses, where it reads, "Jesus returned in the power of the Spirit into Galilee: and there went out a fame of Him through all the region round about. And He taught in their synagogues, being glorified of all." Here we have power in ministry. Now let us glance down to the eighteenth verse: "The Spirit of the Lord is upon me, because He hath anointed me to preach the Gospel." In the thirty-second verse, we read, "They were astonished at His doctrine: for His word was with power."

Jesus did not carry on His ministry in the power of the second Person of the Trinity, but in the anointing of the Holy Spirit, the same power that is at our disposal today. If, therefore, the experience was necessary for Him, how much more so for us!

Now let me impress upon you again the fact that "God anointed Jesus with the Holy Spirit and with power". Has He thus anointed us? Remember also His own words, "The Spirit of the Lord is upon Me because He hath anointed me to preach the Gospel." My brethren, are we able to say the same or are we preaching without the anointing?

The Secret of the Anointing

What is the secret of the Anointing of the Holy Spirit? Does God endue men in a sort of haphazard way? Has He favourites? Are some to be especially blessed irrespective of their qualifications and others passed over? Certainly not. God's difficulty is to find men who are willing to pay the price. There are so few who are ready to stand in the gap. Those who have been specially anointed of the Holy Ghost and whose work reads like a page out of the Acts of the Apostles, did not just happen to stumble on the blessing. They met God. And when we, too, after having counted the cost, are willing to pay the price, God will grant us the same enduement of power from on high.

Now, of course, I am taking it for granted that we are right with God. I mean that there is no known sin in our lives. To seek the anointing of the Spirit before all sin has been confessed and put out of our lives is simply to pound with our fists against a stone wall. God will neither hear nor answer. About this I need say no more. It is self-evident.

And first of all I am persuaded that without an intense *desire and thirst* there will be no real blessing. "I will pour water upon him that is thirsty, and floods upon the dry ground" (Isa. 44:3). There must be a genuine thirst. The ground must realize that it is parched and dry. As long as we are satisfied with our present condition God will not give us anything more. But, "Blessed are they that hunger and thirst after righteousness, for they shall be filled" (Matt.

5:6). "Ye shall seek me and find me when ye shall search for me *with* all your heart" (Jer. 29:13).

As long as I feel that I can somehow or other get on without these special anointings of the Holy Spirit, just so long will God allow me to continue as I am; but as soon as I give up in despair and refuse to be denied, just so soon will He satisfy the hunger and thirst of my heart. Self-sufficiency is the great obstacle. Men have been known to shut themselves in their rooms and refuse to come out or to eat until God met them, so intense has been the desire.

Well now, am I hungry? Do I want the power of the Spirit more than anything else in the world? Am I in earnest about it? Is there a real thirst? Would I be willing to part with all I possess if only I might be a Spirit-anointed worker? How great is my hunger? How strong my desire?

Now the second great prerequisite is *earnest* prayer. So far as I have read the biographies of God's anointed men they have come from their knees with the power of God resting upon them and the fire of the Holy Spirit burning in their souls. I am perfectly confident that the man who does not spend hours alone with God will never know the anointing of the Holy Spirit. The world must be left outside until God alone fills the vision. "These all continued with one accord in prayer and supplication; and suddenly they were all filled with the Holy Ghost" (Acts 1:14; 2:2, 4). "And when they had prayed they were all filled with the Holy Ghost" (Acts 4:31). "Peter and John prayed for them that they might receive the Holy Ghost, and they received the Holy

Ghost" (Acts 8:14–17). Tarry in prayer, earnest, expectant, persevering, united. As someone has well said: "Tarry at the promise till God meets you there." God has promised to answer prayer. It is not that He is unwilling, for the fact is, He is more willing to give than we are to receive. But the trouble is, we are not ready. And only as we wait before Him in prayer can He talk to us, prepare our hearts and get us ready for His glorious power.

Then in the last place there will of course be an *expectant faith.* Everything we receive comes in response to faith. Now there are those who teach that we are simply to "claim" from God, rise believing we have received, and pray no more. That may work sometimes for instantaneous faith is frequently given. But such can also be presumptuous faith which in reality is not faith at all. Receiving by faith means getting an answer. Taking by faith does not mean going without by faith. Real faith always brings a real experience. It is our privilege to tarry before the Lord until the deepest longings and desires of our hearts are satisfied.

Thus we must distinguish between a normal Spirit-filled life, based on surrender and faith, as set forth under "The Fulness of the Spirit," and for which there need be no waiting, except for heart preparation, and repeated *anointings* of the Spirit which come as we tarry in prayer.

In Colossians 4:12 we read: "Epaphras, always labouring fervently for you in prayers, that ye may stand perfect and complete in all the will of God." He did not pray once and then "claim" by faith perfection and completeness in God's will for them, and leave it at that. He laboured fervently in prayers. Note the intensity of his intercessions.

Jesus said: "Tarry until." And so they did not stop praying on the second day and simply "claim" the promised gift of the Holy Ghost by faith; but they continued in prayer "until" they got the answer. To tarry "until" is very different from "claiming" or "taking" by faith, so called.

Elijah did not pray and then "claim" the promised showers. He bowed once, twice, thrice. Yea, he wrestled; he travailed. Seven times he plead, plead "until" the cloud appeared. He tarried until his faith prevailed and then the rain came.

When the Early Church prayed for Peter's release from prison they never thought of asking, claiming, taking, rising and going. But they tarried through the night, determined to get an answer. Yes, they tarried until Peter knocked at the door.

And so with every great revival. Someone tarried, waited, wrestled, travailed "until" he prevailed with God, and the Revival came. And so with the Holy Spirit. The men who have worked in the anointing and unction at some time or other in their lives waited alone with God until they were endued with power from on high.

A Personal Experience

It was in Tampa, Florida, February 10th, 1927. I had delivered a message on The Highest Form of Christian Service; viz., Intercessory Prayer. At the close I called for a season of prayer, and knelt beside the pulpit in the Alliance Tabernacle.

Now I am handicapped for words. How am I going to describe it? What can I say? Nothing was farther from my mind. Not for a moment had I expected anything unusual that morning. But as the people prayed, I was conscious of an unusual Presence. God seemed to hover over the meeting. Presently the blessing began to fall. I was melted, broken, awed, my heart filled with unutterable love; and as my soul rose to meet Him, the tears began to come. I could do nothing but weep and praise my precious, precious Lord. It seemed as though my whole body was bathed in the Holy Ghost, until I was lost in wonder, love and praise. It seemed to me as though I wanted to love everybody. The world and all its troubles faded from my sight. My trials appeared, oh, so insignificant, as God, God Himself filled my whole vision. Oh, it was glorious!

The people saw it. I was conscious of their wonder as they looked up and breathed a "Praise the Lord!" "Hallelujah!" etc. Presently I began to pray, but only exclamations of praise and adoration poured from my lips. I saw no one save Jesus only. As I prayed the audience joined in, some in tones subdued and low, others in ejaculations of thanksgiving. All seemed conscious of God's presence and power. Tears still flowed from my eyes.

After a while I quietly slipped out, and hurried to my room in Rev. John Minder's home. There I saw my mail for which I had been eagerly waiting, lying on the table. But it remained untouched. Back and forth I walked, my face uplifted, my heart thrilled, praising and blessing God. Oh, how near the Saviour was!

As I continued to praise God, the door suddenly opened and a young man came in. I did not give him time to tell me what he wanted, but with quivering voice and yearning heart, I pleaded with him for Christ, and a minute later got him on his knees and poured out my heart in prayer on his behalf. He hardly knew what to think, seemed amazed, and finally went out saying but little. It had been so easy to speak to him just then.

After a while I stopped long enough to glance at my mail. Then, feeling that I could not bear to meet people at the dinner table, I left the house, and wandered I know not where. Every now and again as I walked along the street praising God, the tears would start to my eyes until they became so red that I wondered what the people would think was the matter with me. Time after time I was choked with unutterable outbursts of worship and love that seemed to almost overwhelm me. I sang, deep down in my soul, my own chorus:

> *Alone, dear Lord, ah yes, alone with Thee!*
> *My aching heart at rest, my spirit free;*
> *My sorrow gone, my burdens all forgotten,*
> *When far away I soar alone with Thee.*

I seemed shut in with God. For a while as I walked I would think of something else, but in a moment my thoughts would fly back to God, and again the tears gushed forth as my heart was melted, humbled and broken in His presence. At last I wended my way back home with a sweet, settled peace in my heart and a light that never shone on land or sea in my soul. The glow passed, but the fragrance remained. I did not speak in tongues and I never have, but I had a foretaste of what shall be hereafter. Oh, how I love and adore Him! Jesus, my Lord, my God!

Have You the Burden?

Alexander Duff, that veteran missionary to India, went home to Scotland to die. In great feebleness he stood before the Presbyterian Assembly, and pleaded for missionaries for India. In the midst of his appeal he fainted, and was taken into another room. After physicians had worked over him for some time, he finally recovered consciousness, and when he realized where he was, he said, "I didn't finish my appeal; take me back and let me finish it." But they told him he could do it only at the peril of his life. He said, "I'll do it if I die."

So they led back that white-haired veteran into the Assembly hall, and as he appeared at the door, they all sprang to their feet as one man to greet him, and then sat down and listened in tearful and breathless silence to that grand old hero of the cross.

With trembling voice he said, "Fathers and mothers of Scotland, is it true that you have no more sons to send to India? There is money in the bank to send them, but where are the labourers who will go into the field? When Queen Victoria calls for volunteers for her army in India, you freely give your sons, and say nothing about the trying climate of that land. But when the Lord Jesus calls for volunteers, you say, 'We have no more sons to give.'"

Then turning to the Moderator of the Assembly, he said, "Mr. Moderator, if it is true that Scotland has no more sons to give to Christ for India, then, although I lost my health in that land and came home to die, I will be off to-morrow, and go back to the shores of the Ganges and lay my life down as a witness for Christ, to let them know that there is at least one Scotsman who is ready to die for them."

Why did he act so? What was it that made Alexander Duff create such a scene? Had his mind failed? Was he mentally deranged? By no means. Well, then, what was it? Ah! it was his passion, his love for souls. The burden of India's perishing millions lay heavily upon him, and the love of Christ constrained him. How then could he do otherwise?

And in that thrilling episode, beloved, you have the result of the anointing, the evidence of the fulness of the Holy Ghost. For when a man has been "endued with power from on high" he will have a burden for souls. This, then, is the climax, the acid test. Tell it not that you are filled unless you have this burden. Boast no more of your anointing if you love not souls.

Oh, my brother, tell me: nay! tell God: Have you the burden? Do you know the passion of which I speak? Are you haunted day and night with the thought that millions are perishing on every side, that multitudes are going down to the regions of despair, "without one ray of hope or light, with future dark as endless night"? Does the Holy Spirit awaken you during the silent hours of sleep, to intercede on behalf of lost men and women? Have you ever agonized over the perishing? Do you know anything about soul-travail? When last did you wrestle with God for dear ones out of Christ? For, mark you, if you have been truly anointed of the Holy Ghost, such will be your experience.

It was thus that the Spirit came upon John Knox and made him cry: "Oh, God, give me Scotland, or I die!" So also He came upon John Wesley causing him to write: "You have nothing to do but to save souls," and giving him such a burden that tens of thousands were snatched as brands from the burning. Later He anointed Chas. G. Finney, anointed him so mightily that every one to whom he spoke that first epoch-making day, turned to God; and then made him the centre of revivals that witnessed the conversions of untold multitudes. That same burden made D. L. Moody, under the mighty anointing of the Spirit, exclaim: "The world has yet to see what God can do through one man wholly surrendered to Him," so that Moody placed one foot on Europe and the other on America and shook both continents for God. General Booth knew the burden, and from London's slums and haunts of vice, he sought and won sinners of the darkest dye. John Smith stained his room with his tears for lost souls. Edward Payson wore the boards at the side of his bed by his knees where he agonized and travailed for lost men and women. It was that same passion for souls that made William Bramwell wrestle with God for thirty-six hours in a sand-pit, without a morsel of food.

Ah, that burden, that burden for souls – how it has characterized God's anointed ones all down the centuries! Paul, Carvasso, Oxtoby, Whitefield, Stoner, McCheyne, Brainerd, Bounds, Hyde, and a host of others, mighty wrestlers with God. Theirs, my brethren, is the experience I crave above all other, for they had God's seal. There was no doubt about their anointing; they were Spirit-filled, every last one of them, for they travailed in soul for the perishing.

"Ye shall receive power, after that the Holy Ghost is come upon you: and ye shall be witnesses unto Me" (Acts 1:8). Thus spoke Jesus. The purpose then of the enduement of power is witnessing. That was to be the supreme result; not another thing is mentioned. And the objective of witnessing, of course, is the salvation of souls. So that he who is truly endued becomes a witness. And, mark you, we are to be witnesses unto Him. "Ye shall be witnesses unto me," said Jesus. Not to a doctrine, nor an experience; not to a blessing, nor a special gift; but to a Person, the crucified Christ. Unless therefore we are consumed with a passion for souls, unless the burden for the lost is ours, there is no evidence that we have been anointed or that we are Spirit-filled.

There are four great results that follow the anointing, four evidences that can neither be disputed nor counterfeited. The first is victory over sin; the second, power in service ; the third, the fruit of the Spirit; and the fourth, a burden for souls. Now I care not what else you may have received, even though visions and revelations have been yours – they fade into insignificance in the face of these four tremendous results.

Have you, then, the burden? Do you weep over souls? Are you longing to see them saved? Do you value all meetings only in so far as they contribute to the salvation of sinners? Do you judge of the spirituality of a Church by its interest in the saving of lost men and women? Or, are you glorying in some great emotional experience, some ecstatic thrill, physical or otherwise, more than in the salvation of the perishing?

Seek not the anointing for your own happiness. Ask not for the fulness in order that you may boast of a thrilling experience. But seek rather a baptism into Christ's sufferings, and ask for the burden that produces soul-travail, and you will not be disappointed. Thus you will know when you are filled and anointed. Unmistakable evidence will be yours. Neglect it not, but dare to go the Calvary way and bleed for the lost.

> *Oh for a heart that weeps o'er souls,*
>   *Weeps with a love in anguish born!*
> *Oh for a broken, contrite heart,*
>   *A heart for sinners rent and torn!*

Oh for the pangs of Calv'ry's death,
  In fellowship with Thee, my Lord!
Oh for the death that lives in life,
  And bleeds for those who spurn Thy Word!

Naught have I sought of blessing, Lord,
  Save that which brings lost souls to Thee;
All else is vain, nor dare I boast—
  This lord, I crave, be this my plea.

Have Thou Thy way whate'er the cost,
  In death I live, in life I die;
Thy way, not mine, dear Lord, I pray,
  Souls, precious souls, my ceaseless cry.

5

The Leading of the Spirit

"As they ministered to the Lord, and fasted, the Holy Ghost said, 'Separate me Barnabas and Saul for the work whereunto I have called them.' And when they had fasted and prayed, and laid their hands on them, they sent them away. So they, being sent forth by the Holy Ghost, departed" (Acts 13:2–4).

He Calls Barnabas and Saul

Thus the Holy Ghost called Barnabas and Saul, and thus He calls men today. That is, if they are listening, if they are quiet before Him, if they have placed themselves at His disposal, and are led by Him. Barnabas and Saul, you see, were ministering to the Lord; they were praying and fasting. The world had been shut out. They were waiting to know the mind of the Spirit. When God's children get into that attitude the Holy Ghost can make known His will and call those whom God chooses.

But we are so busy. There is so much rush and hurry. We have never learned the importance of being still before Him. He cannot get our ear. We are unable to hear His voice. Hence, we think we are in God's will, we hope our plan will be His, and we go at our own bidding and fail. Yet all the time the blessed Holy Ghost, a Person, with power to choose, speak and send, the One who ought to be recognized as Commander in our lives, is waiting, longing, eager to make known God's plan for our ministry. But we will not hear.

Oh how active was the Holy Ghost in the days of the Early Church! But that was because He was given His rightful place and recognized as the One in charge of the work. How inactive He seems to be today. And all because He has been slighted and ignored. Man's plans have claimed preference over His. Man's programme has gotten in His way. Self has usurped His place. Hence, He can no longer choose and call, equip and send. But, beloved, He is willing, and this is still His work. He knows us all by name. Oh may we yield to Him, and obey, that God's programme may yet be carried out!

What a revival followed! Oh how churches sprang up! Souls saved everywhere. The Gospel the power of God unto salvation on every hand. Saints established and built up in the Faith. And all because the Holy Ghost was recognized, and His orders obeyed. Thank God, it can be so again. He is still looking for men, men who will yield implicit obedience. And when He finds a man who will quietly wait until he gets his orders, who will listen to no voice but His, who will be guided by none save the Holy Ghost, who will hear His call, and go forth at His command – ah, then there will be blessing indeed.

He Leads Philip

"Then the Spirit said unto Philip, Go near, and join thyself to this chariot. And Philip ran" (Acts 8:29, 30).

Again the Spirit speaks, for He is in command, and He has a willing, obedient servant through whom to do His work. Of course, He could have done it in a thousand other ways. But He chooses men; He equips men; and men He uses. Not means but men. Not programmes but men. Not organizations but men. Not movements but men. Not machinery but men. Not Committees and Boards but Spirit-filled, Spirit-taught, Spirit-led men.

So He chooses Philip, takes him away from a great revival, where humanly speaking he is badly needed, and sends him to the solitude of the desert. Yet Philip never questions, never asks: "Why am I here? What is there to do in this place? Had I not better get back to Samaria and help the brethren there?" No, he just trusts his Leader, for the Holy Ghost, he knows, makes no mistakes.

Of course there are chariots passing every now and then, but what are they in comparison to the great crowds he had left? But Philip, ever dependent on the Spirit, prays, and commences to ask God if he has anything to do with these chariots. You see, he is willing to be led. But the chariots continue to pass and God is silent. Until suddenly a chariot with a single occupant, a black man, passes by. And like a flash the Spirit speaks: "Go near, and join thyself to this chariot." Not to the others, note, but to "this" one. Ah! God knows His worker, and God also knows those who will respond, those who are hungry. God wastes no time, and makes no mistakes.

"And Philip *ran.*" Oh how eager he was! How delighted to do his Master's bidding! The Spirit spoke, he ran. What perfect co-operation! Do you see now why God doesn't use all the same? Who today is on the tip-toe of expectancy, ready, yea, eager to be off at the Spirit's bidding? Do we run to obey? Or do we complain and grumble at our task? Philip *ran.* What about us? It is still our privilege to be guided directly by the Holy Ghost. We, too, may hear His voice. But – will we obey?

He was ready, this black man. The Spirit had seen to that. He was even reading the book of Isaiah, and especially the passage about Christ. Everything was timed to a second. The Spirit got the Ethiopian ready and then He had Philip ready. My! what a General! And so Philip found a hungry heart and won a soul to Christ. Then on he went rejoicing, and all because the Holy Ghost had one man upon whom He could depend. And He's just the same today.

He Forbids Paul

"Forbidden of the Holy Ghost to preach the Word in Asia." . . . "They assayed to go into Bithynia; but the Spirit suffered them not." . . . "Come over into Macedonia, and help us" (Acts 16:6, 9).

Ah, here's another kind of guidance, is it not? Orders from the Holy Ghost to forbear. It is one thing when the *King* or ruler of a country forbids; it is quite another when that One is the Holy Ghost.

There is no situation with which He is not familiar. To Him no country is unknown. The problems and difficulties He has already foreseen. The Holy Ghost is never taken by surprise. Hence, if He forbids there is a real reason for it. We do not need to know why, it is enough that He, our Leader, has barred the way. He has some other purpose which in His own time will be made clear.

Paul decided to take the Gospel into Asia. The Spirit forbade him. Then he endeavoured to get into Bithynia, and the Holy Ghost blocked the way. What to do next he knew not. But that night decided him. For he saw a vision; he heard a Call: "Come over into Macedonia, and help us." The door was open and he went. It was the Spirit's leading, and all was well.

Oh, beloved, faint not when doors are shut. For if you are in God's will, He will Himself unlock the bars and let you in, or else He will keep the way closed and later lead you in another direction. Pray and wait. Fret not nor complain. The Spirit knows God's purpose, You have received Him; He is your Leader, your Guide, and He never errs. The vision will come at last. "Though it tarry, wait for it." "He that believeth shall not make haste." Trust even in the dark. God will not be unmindful. He never forgets.

How well I remember passing through the experience of the closed door! How firmly barred it seemed to be. No effort of mine could open it. And so I waited and prayed. Other spheres of service invited, some of them most attractive, but I heeded not. God, I knew, would open the door. But it was long shut. Two years and more He tried me. He knew that I needed the furnace of affliction, and He wanted to give me a deeper training for His work. And so He kept the door closed, until at last His hour struck, His time came. And in the most natural way in the world, without any effort of my own, the door opened and I entered.

Dear one, why not let Him guide? Why not recognize the Holy Ghost? Why not stop making mistakes and missing the way? No one else can take His place. He and He alone can be your Guide. Then confess your negligence and henceforth honour the Holy Ghost, who alone can lead you aright.

6

The Keeper of the Keys

Suppose you buy a house. Instead of getting all the keys at once, you get but one or two. You are given access, let us say, to the living-room only. Now, the home is yours. You own it. It belongs to you and to you alone, but you can only enter one room, and so there you live. The other doors are all securely locked. You are in the house, but in one room only. You have by no means possessed your possessions.

So it is with the Holy Spirit. You belong to Him and He is there. He dwells within. But He is only on the threshold of your life. He has not taken complete possession, and all because you will not give Him the other keys. Hence, He has to remain, as it were, in the living-room. He can get no farther. Not because He is not willing, but because you will not let Him. The other rooms of your heart are closed against Him. He has never possessed you. You are not filled.

And why? Well, perhaps because you have not been taught. Or possibly because there are things in the other rooms of your heart that you do not want Him to see. You prefer to live your own life. So far as the living-room is concerned you are glad to have Him. That is your public life. But the other rooms are private. And there are shelves behind the doors that you would be ashamed to have Him scrutinize. There are things in your life that you are not willing to surrender. Hence He is barred.

Now, to return to our illustration, there comes a day when you are given all the keys, and at last you are able to enter all the rooms. For the first time you are really in control. Every room is open to you and you go where you like. You can arrange the furniture to suit your taste. You begin by house cleaning. And, oh, how the dust flies! For a while there is plenty of commotion, a real disturbance. But finally every room is clean and your house made fit to live in. You are now in complete possession.

So it is with the Holy Spirit. There comes a day in your life when you give Him all the keys and ask Him to enter every room. It may be at some great spiritual Convention, through the reading of a book, or as the result of a sudden tragedy that drives you to God. Be that as it may, the crisis takes place and you yield. One by one He unlocks the doors, examines each room and begins at once to set things right. Everything displeasing goes. Only what He approves is left. Sins that you could not overcome are now conquered, for He is in command. Thus He fills.

But will there be any manifestation, you ask, any special demonstration or commotion? That depends on the condition He finds. If He has been kept on the threshold for long, and you give up the keys all at once, well, something is bound to happen as He takes possession. Or, if you have allowed a lot of dust to accumulate, if the shelves behind the doors are laden with many things that are displeasing to God, and if there is some real house-cleaning to be done, again there will be considerable commotion. The dust will fly. And until the house has been thoroughly cleaned and everything set right, there will be upheavals that will never be forgotten.

But if, on the other hand, you have already let Him into several rooms, and have only withheld one or two, it may be, as it was with F. B. Meyer and Charles Inwood, that He will very quietly occupy the territory. In other words, if you have always walked in the light and it has been more a lack of instruction than anything else, then He may come as the soft gentle showers, and the only manifestation will be a deeper peace, a richer and fuller realization of His presence.

Will there be two experiences? It would seem so. But should not one follow so closely on the other that they will be remembered as one? Is it God's plan that we should wander for forty years in the wilderness? Or does He want us to leave Egypt and go straight through, right into Canaan? Why should we linger by the way? Why wander at all? Is He not able to take us through? Most assuredly.

The children of Israel failed. Hence, they remembered two distinct experiences, the Red Sea and the Jordan River. And these experiences were forty years apart. Whereas they could have happened within less than two weeks of each other, and then they never would have remembered the great gap between. One should have immediately followed the other.

And so with us. From the day of our conversion we should live Spirit-filled, sanctified, victorious Christian lives. But, oh, how few do! With most of us there is a wilderness experience, a time of back-sliding and wandering – wasted years. Yet, even now, thank God, we may return. Oh, then, let us hasten again to Kadesh Barnea. Let us even now cross the Jordan and enter in. Let us yield to the Holy Spirit, give Him all the keys and bid Him take possession.

And rest assured, beloved, that there will be no waiting, no delay. As soon as a vacuum is created the air rushes in. And "how much more" is God's Word regarding the Holy Spirit. He is far more willing to fill than you are to be filled. Never has He kept you waiting. It is you who have kept Him. The only delay necessary, so far as He is concerned, will be the time it takes you to yield and obey. If you have to tarry it will be because you will not surrender the keys.

The Spirit-filled life is God's ideal for every believer. He wants to possess you, and the moment you surrender the territory, He will occupy it. When you are willing He will move in. For He will never be satisfied until He is in control. He must be the Keeper of the Keys.

7

The Comforter

"And I will pray the Father, and He shall give you another Comforter, that He may abide with you forever" (John 14:16). "The *Comforter,* which is the Holy Ghost" (John 14:26). "The *Comforter,* even the Spirit of truth" (John 15:26). "If I go not away, the *Comforter* will not come" (John 16:7).

Beloved, do you know the Comforter? I don't mean intellectually, but experimentally. It is one thing to believe in Jesus Christ with the head, but it is quite another thing to believe with the heart. It is one thing to give an intellectual assent to the truth concerning the Holy Spirit, while it is quite another thing to believe experimentally. From the first I most firmly believed and proclaimed the personality of the Holy Ghost, so plainly taught in the Bible. But not until that never-to-be-forgotten day when God revealed Him to my spirit did I believe experimentally. Only as God quickens you to apprehend the Holy Ghost as a Person will you enter into the heart experience of this precious truth. God must reveal Him.

It is not until you are thus awakened to believe in your heart that He ever becomes real to you. But, oh what a Comforter He is when you know Him experimentally! How He soothes and quiets! How near, how dear and precious! No earthly friend so close to you. All that Jesus ever was He is, the Paraclete in very deed. Ah, beloved, do you know Him thus? Have you found in Him a Comforter? Is He as real to you as Jesus Himself?

How He Met Me

I was at the cross-roads when He met me. I knew not which way to turn. The battle had been unusually severe, the assaults of the enemy terrible. I could not drive him away. My heart was lonely. I was fearfully homesick and longed to get back to my family and my work. Then – He revealed Himself. It was in Truro, N.S., July 13th, 1928. At once my heart was filled to overflowing. I walked the room and praised God in the joy of the Holy Ghost. My fears were gone and the struggle over. The attack of Satan was frustrated, and that with no effort of mine. I was simply filled with Him.

Regarding the future my heart was at rest. The homesickness passed away. I was no longer anxious to get back. Every hour was occupied with Him. Peace like a river flowed over my soul. All murmuring and complaining ceased. I was satisfied to wait God's time. The Comforter was with me. He was my thought day and night. I wrote of Him, sang of Him, worshipped and praised Him.

Jesus promised Him. It was expedient, He said, that He should go in order that the Comforter might come. In His flesh He could be in but one place at a time, whereas the Comforter could be in all God's children to the very end. And so He has been all down the centuries. In the midst of sorrow and persecution, He has been present. But just in proportion as He is recognized and honoured does He manifest Himself to each one individually.

Temptation

Oh, what a Comforter He is! How He quiets the storms! What victories He wins! Temptations that seemed irresistible vanish before His power. Passions that nothing else could quell subside at His command. Sins that the flesh could never hope to overcome lose all their strength when He, the Holy Ghost, controls. And oh, the comfort, the relief from the unequal conflict! How He comforts the tempted soul!

You have fallen. It is your old besetting sin. Again and again you have failed God. Each time there has been penitence and sorrow and each time new resolutions and vows. Yet in spite of all, you have yielded. Finally, you turn as a drowning man in the darkness of despair to Him. The blood cleanses. The Spirit fills. You are forgiven, emancipated and established. But you can't forgive yourself. You can't forget. The memory of lost ideals haunts and torments you. At last there comes a deeper experience, and you lose yourself in Him. Sweetly He works, heals the broken heart, binds up the wounds. A new Presence possesses you – the Comforter. And so the day breaks, and all the shadows flee away.

Criticism

You have been pained. Friends have said bitter things against you. And, oh how they have hurt! "Yea, mine own familiar friend, in whom I trusted, which did eat of my bread, hath lifted up his heel against me" (Ps. 41:9). Slanderous reports have been circulated about you. And through it all, as a dumb sheep taught of God, you have refrained from opening your mouth. At last, perchance, God has judged.

Meanwhile the furnace experience through which you are passing is proving a blessing in disguise. For in the fellowship of His sufferings you are beginning to know the comfort of Another. The Holy Ghost, no longer a vague, mysterious influence, now becomes a living, bright reality. Oh how He soothes the wounded heart! How tenderly He whispered to you, "Peace, be still." And as you rest in His eternal calm, though the darts fly thick and fast, you can afford to rejoice, for you know that all is well.

Loneliness

Perhaps you have had to dwell alone, far, far from those you loved. The loneliness was unendurable, the solitude a daily torture. You felt as though you could not face another day. Or perchance it was a memory out of the dim shadows of the forgotten past – a dream that never came true. And then, years went by; other experiences were yours, but – you never could forget. And as you recalled the vision of those far-off days, your heart ached, and you knew what it was to be lonely, oh so lonely!

Then God quickened your spirit to an experimental apprehension of the Holy Ghost. You recognized Him, and placed yourself absolutely at His disposal. And He, He revealed Himself to you as the Comforter, for you needed comfort. Now you were no longer lonely. You had Another with you, and He was there constantly, day and night. Your first thought in the morning was of Him, and your last at night. He became real, oh so real, He, the Holy Ghost, the Comforter.

Bereavement

Darkness! Midnight! The last farewell said, the final handclasp given, and the dear one whom you love as your own life, has slipped away, and you are left in utter desolation, bereaved. With aching heart, like one in a dream, you go through the horrible ordeal of the funeral, the interment. As you turn away from the cold, silent grave that holds all you loved and cherished on earth, you sob aloud in your agony and wonder how you can ever live on.

The days come and the days go; while the long, dark night, when all is still and a thousand visions of the dear face flit before your wearied brain, only increases your suffering and brings no relief. Friends cannot help. Even in religion you are disappointed. The Church fails to comfort. God seems far away. "Oh, for the touch of a vanished hand, and the sound of a voice that is still!" is your agonizing cry.

But at last one day – and oh, what a day! – you hear about the Comforter, the One sent for just such an experience as yours. At first you grope in darkness, knowing not how to appropriate Him. You commence to read the words of Jesus, especially His promises about Another whom He was to send. "And I will pray the Father, and He shall give you another Comforter, that He may abide with you forever" (John 14:16). Immediately your attention is arrested. "Can it be," you wonder, "that this is what I need? Oh, if only I knew how to get it!" How to get *it*! But you read again. Presently the light breaks. Not it, but *Him*.

Suddenly God quickens your spiritual understanding, and before long you are rejoicing in Him, the Comforter. And to your amazement, your sorrow is gone, the heartache has ceased, your mind is on Another. Immediately you remember your loss, but the tears that flow are now tears of gratitude and praise, tears of joy in the Holy Ghost. The dear one has not returned, no, but Another, the Comforter, has filled your heart, and become more to you than all else beside. The vacancy is still there, yet strangely occupied, and all is well. Oh, what a Comforter.

Thus it was with the Early Church. "Walking in the *comfort* of the Holy Ghost" (Acts 9:31). He was the Comforter then, He Will be now. Without Him, how hard the task; but with Him, how easy! Beloved, you need Him. In fact, you cannot get along without Him. Why go through life and miss God's best?

8

The Sevenfold Work of the Spirit

There are seven words that describe the work of the Holy Spirit in the life of the believer. They are the *Baptism,* the *Gift,* the *Indwelling,* the *Sealing, the Earnest,* the *Filling* and the *Anointing* of the Spirit. Let us study them one by one.

1. *The Baptism of the Spirit*

"For by one Spirit are we all baptized into one body, whether we be Jews or Gentiles, whether we be bond or free" (1 Cor. 12:13).

Note, if you will, that we are *all* baptized. Not one here and there; not those who have met certain conditions, but all – every member of the body of Christ. There is but one baptism. (Eph. 4:5).

In other words, the Holy Spirit takes a Jew here and a Gentile there, regenerates him and places him in the Body of Christ, the Church. Thus the sinner who believes on Christ is baptized by the Spirit into the one Body. And thus the Church is formed.

That experience, therefore, takes place at the time of conversion, and is already past so far as the believer is concerned, and it is never repeated.

2. *The Gift of the Spirit*

"God gave them the like Gift as He did unto us" (Acts 11:17). "On the Gentiles also was poured out the Gift of the Holy Ghost." (Acts 10:45).

Until Cornelius the Spirit was given after water baptism or by the laying on of hands. But when he, the first Gentile, was converted, the Holy Spirit was given without waiting, without water baptism, without the laying on of hands or any other condition than simple faith in Christ the moment he believed. That is the order today. See notes in Scofield Bible on Acts 10:44 and 19:2.

Peter never again proclaimed Acts 2:38, so far as the record goes. Paul never preached it. And no evangelist would ever dream of preaching it today. Since Paul's New Revelation the message has been Acts 16:31.

The dispensation of water baptism "for the remission of sins" as a pre-requisite for the receiving of the Gift of the Spirit, which was the Kingdom message and had to do with the Jews only, ended with Paul's New Revelation of the Gospel of the Grace of God for sinners – Faith plus nothing.

Therefore, every believer has received the Gift of the Holy Spirit.

3. *The Indwelling of the Spirit*

"Know ye not that ye are the temple of God, and that the Spirit of God *dwelleth* in you?" (1 Cor. 3:16).

And here we have the truth of the indwelling.

Having been baptized by the Holy Spirit into the Body of Christ, and having received the Gift of the Holy Ghost, He now indwells each and every believer.

4. *The Sealing of the Spirit*

"After that ye believed, ye were sealed with that Holy Spirit of promise" (Eph. 1:13).

The sealing of the Holy Spirit denotes three things: first, a finished transaction, second, ownership, and third, security.

First, a finished transaction, "'Tis done, the great transaction's done, I am my Lord's and He is mine." The believer has been saved. The transaction has been completed and the work done. And the moment he is saved, he is sealed.

Second, ownership. He now belongs to God. He is God's property. He has changed owners. Satan no longer has any rights so far as he is concerned. He has a new Master – God.

Third, security. Having been sealed, he is secure. God will never let him go. "I give unto them eternal life," He says; "and they shall never perish." He has been saved for time and eternity, and he is safe in the Father's keeping.

My father was a station agent, and it was his duty to seal and break the seals on cars. No one else was allowed to touch them. When the car had been loaded he sealed it. That seal denoted a finished transaction. The work had been done. It indicated that the car belonged to the Company, for it was the

Company's seal that he placed on it. Furthermore, it was a pledge of security. The contents of the car were safe. No one dare break the seal.

And so it is with the believer. As soon as he is saved, he is sealed by the Holy Ghost, the Spirit Himself being the seal. That means that he has been born again, that he is God's child, and that God guarantees his safety.

Thus the sealing of the Spirit has already taken place in the life of the believer.

5. *The Earnest of the Spirit*

"That Holy Spirit of promise, which is the *earnest* of our inheritance until the redemption of the purchased possession" (Eph. 1:13, 14).

"God; who hath also sealed us, and given the *earnest* of the Spirit in our hearts" (2 Cor. 1:21, 22).

The earnest, or the deposit, the guarantee of what is to follow, the foretaste. A man buys my home. He gives me a small deposit to bind the bargain. That deposit is but a little of what is finally to be mine. It is his guarantee that he will pay the balance. I take it and rejoice. I know that some day I will get it all.

Thank God for the foretaste of glory that is ours. Even that is about all we can contain now. If the earnest is so glorious, what will the full inheritance be! If the presence of Jesus is so wonderful now, what will it be when we see Him face to face! If the raindrops are so precious, how glorious will be the showers!

The earnest, therefore, is ours now. We have had it

already; we are having it still as we walk in the light, and we will have it until at last we enter His presence.

6. *The Filling of the Spirit*

"Be filled with the Spirit" (Eph. 5:18).

"Be being filled," as it is in the original. We are to be filled, and then filled again, and again and again. And so we come to the truth that is specially for us today.

Every true believer has been baptized by the Spirit, as we have seen; he has received the gift of the Holy Ghost; he is indwelt by the Spirit; he has been sealed, and he has the earnest. But not every believer is filled. Hence, the command, "Be filled with the Spirit."

As we turn to Christ, from sin; as we yield ourselves, body, soul and spirit, to do His will, He fills us with the Holy Ghost, and we are enabled to live Spirit-filled lives. Thus we become fruit-bearing Christians.

This experience is, therefore, continuous from the time we believe until we see Him as He is. In most lives, however, there is an initial crisis experience, and in some, many. All do not fully yield at the time of conversion. But when they do, He fills. And the Spirit-filled life becomes the normal life of the believer.

7. *The Anointing of the Spirit*

"The Spirit of the Lord is upon me, because He hath *anointed* me to preach the Gospel to the poor; He hath sent me to heal the broken-hearted, to preach deliverance to the captives, and recovering of sight to the blind, to set at liberty them that are bruised, to preach the acceptable year of the Lord" (Luke 4:18, 19), see Acts 10:38.

Here, my friend, is the work of the minister. To do it Jesus Christ was anointed. Have you, too, been anointed? If your ministry is to be effective, you must be an anointed man.

You are to preach the Gospel. You are to bring comfort to the broken-hearted. Satan's slaves must be set free. Men spiritually blind must be made to see. Souls in bondage to sin, their lives wrecked and ruffled, must be saved. You must be able to bring men to an immediate decision in this, God's day of grace.

Can you do it? Not unless you are Spirit-anointed. It is a big order for any man. And only the enabling power of the Spirit will suffice.

All down the centuries God has anointed His servants. He came upon Samson, Elijah and Elisha. He came on Jesus, Peter and Paul. On Wesley and Whitfield. On Brainerd, Edwards and Finney. And He came on Roberts, Spurgeon and Moody. And when He did, He wrought mightily through them.

For these men tarried before the Lord in prayer. They wrestled in intercession. They agonized for souls. And as they did, the Spirit came upon them and thousands were swept into the Kingdom.

You, my friend, may never be a Moody or a Wesley. But God will use you to the full limit of your capacity, for He is no respecter of persons. Oh then, wait before Him; spend much time alone with God; agonize for souls, and you will be anointed with the Spirit of God.

9

The Outpouring on the Moravians

One of the greatest Outpourings of the Spirit since the days of the Apostles occurred on Wednesday morning, August 13th, 1727, among the Moravian Brethren at Herrnhut, Germany, on the estate of Count Zinzendorf, in Saxony.

For years the followers of John Huss, the martyred Bohemian Reformer, had endured persecution and death. Fleeing from imprisonment and torture, they at last found a refuge in Germany where Count Zinzendorf, a young Christian nobleman, offered them an asylum on his estates.

Zinzendorf, who at the age of four drew up and signed the following covenant: "Dear Saviour, do Thou be mine, and I will be Thine," stood one day in the Dusseldorf Gallery before a picture of the Christ, painted, as so well described in the little tract, "The Artist and the Gipsy Girl," underneath which were the words:

This have I done for Thee,
What doest Thou for Me?

Turning from the glittering allurements of Paris, he there and then gave himself utterly to Christ, adopting as his motto:

I have one passion; it is Jesus, Jesus, only.

Speaking of what occurred that memorable thirteenth day of August, historians tell that they left the House of God "hardly knowing whether they belonged to earth or had already gone to Heaven".

Zinzendorf, in his description of it, says: "The Saviour permitted to come upon us a Spirit of Whom we had hitherto not had any experience or knowledge. Hitherto WE had been the leaders and helpers. Now the Holy Spirit Himself took full control of everything and everybody."

All are agreed that it was a definite, unmistakable Outpouring of the Holy Spirit on the entire congregation, so wonderful that it was absolutely indescribable.

The Brethren had been judging one another; doctrinal disputes were common; heated arguments that threatened division and discord were the order of the day. Instead of love, bitterness. Instead of brotherly unity, strife.

"When God intends great mercy for His peoples," says Matthew Henry, "the first thing He does is to set them a-praying." And so it was at Herrnhut. The more spiritual among them, utterly dissatisfied with themselves, commenced to cry mightily to God for help. That their prayer was answered, there is abundant proof. James Montgomery, their greatest hymn-writer, gives the following realistic description:

They walked with God in Peace and Love,
But failed with one another;
While sternly for the Faith they strove,
Brother fell out with brother;
But He in whom they put their trust,
Who knew their frames that they were dust,
Pitied and healed their weakness.

He found them in His House of Prayer,
With one accord assembled;
And so revealed His Presence there,
They wept with joy and trembled:
One cup they drank, one bread they brake,
One baptism shared, one language spake,
Forgiving and forgiven.

We are apt to think of the glorious Methodist Awakening as the greatest since Pentecost. But we must trace Methodism to its source. And its source was the Moravian Revival of 1727. For through the Moravians both John and Charles Wesley come into the Light. And much of their theology they got from the Moravian Brethren. Then out of Methodism came the Salvation Army and scores of other spiritual movements.

So that to the Moravians belongs the credit for all, and for the Moravians, Count Zinzendorf and John Huss. Through Count Zinzendorf God set in motion spiritual currents that have revolutionized the world. It is doubtful if any other man has been so mightily used since the days of the Apostle Paul. Had it not been for him there might never have been a Moravian Church of unparalleled missionary fame, nor a Methodist Church with its Wesleys, nor a Salvation Army with its Booths.

What now were the experiences and what the results of this unique Outpouring of the Holy Spirit on the Moravian Brethren? As for the experiences, there were two that stood out in bold relief, and as for the results, again there were two that have amazed all Christendom. First, then, the two experiences, and second, the results.

*

The first experience that they constantly emphasized and that was passed on through Wesley to the Methodists was

A Definite Knowledge of *Salvation by Faith in Christ Alone*

They made the discovery that the Church could not save them; that there was no salvation in its creeds, doctrines or dogmas; that good works, moral living, commandment keeping, praying and Bible reading, could not avail; much less culture, character or conduct. They found out that Christ alone could save; that He was willing and able to receive sinners at a moment's notice; that justification, the forgiveness of sins, the new birth, etc., were instantaneous experiences received the very moment a sinner believed on Christ; that salvation was through grace and by faith, apart from the deeds of the law; that when a man is saved he has peace with God, and that he receives the Assurance of salvation by the witness of the Holy Spirit in his heart.

Thus pardon is sought and obtained through the merits of the shed blood alone and solely upon the ground of the finished work of Jesus Christ. A knowledge or assurance of sins forgiven is absolutely essential. This definite assurance is given by the Holy Spirit. Salvation is thus an instantaneous experience.

It was this definite experience of salvation that made both the Moravians and the early Methodists so bold and fearless in their proclamation of the Gospel to both high and low, at home and in heathen lands.

In the oldest Moravian hymn known, written by John Huss himself, the father of the Moravian Brethren, in the year 1400, several years before his martyrdom, we have the seeds planted that for a while seemed to die, and then in 1727 bore such a sudden and abundant harvest:

> *To avert from men God's wrath*
> *Jesus suffered in our stead.*
> *By an ignominious death*
> *He a full atonement made;*
> *And by His own Precious blood*
> *Brought us, sinners, nigh to God.*
>
> *But examine first your case,*
> *Whether you be in the faith;*
> *Do you long for pard'ning grace?*

> *Is your only hope His death?*
> *Then, howe'er your soul's opprest,*
> *Come, you are a worthy guest.*

The finest illustrations of this glorious truth are found in the conversions of John and Charles Wesley, both of whom were led into the light by Peter Boehler, later a Moravian bishop. Speaking of John Wesley, Boehler wrote, "He wept bitterly and asked me to pray for him. I can truly affirm that he is a poor, heart-broken sinner, hungering after a better righteousness."

But at last Wesley, destined to become the mightiest revivalist since Paul, found Christ. And after years of faithful service we find him giving expression on his dying bed to this great personal experience of salvation:

> *I the chief of sinners am,*
> *But Jesus died for me.*

Peter Boehler's dealings with Charles Wesley were even more startling. Following is Charles Wesley's most illuminating statement:

"He asked me, 'Do you hope to be saved?' 'Yes.' 'For what reason do you hope it?' 'Because I have used my *best endeavours* to serve God.' He shook his head and said no more. I thought him very uncharitable, saying in my heart, 'What? Are not my *endeavours* a sufficient ground of hope? Would he rob me of my *endeavours?* I have nothing else to trust to.'"

Thus this faithful Moravian soul-winner probed

the soul of Charles Wesley, an Oxford graduate and an Anglican missionary, until at last he, too, accepted Christ by faith, having made the discovery that *his best endeavours* were not a sufficient ground for hope.

And now, with this new and vital experience of salvation, Charles Wesley was able to sing:

> *He breaks the power of cancelled sin,*
> *He sets the Prisoner free;*
> *His blood can make the foulest clean,*
> *His blood availed for me.*

So, too, in that matchless hymn, so full of Moravian theology, "Arise, my soul, arise!"

> *Five bleeding wounds He bears,*
> *Received on Calvary;*
> *They pour effectual prayers,*
> *They strongly plead for me:*
> *"Forgive him, oh forgive," they cry,*
> *"Nor let that ransomed sinner die."*
>
> *The Father hears Him pray,*
> *His dear anointed One;*
> *He cannot turn away*
> *The presence of His Son;*
> *The Spirit answers to the blood*
> *And tells me I am born of God.*

Others, too, gave expression to it. This is how John Cennick put it:

> *I'll point to Thy redeeming Blood,*
> *And say, "Behold the way to God!"*

And oh, with what certainty, assurance and holy boldness was it proclaimed by Count Zinzendorf himself:

> *The Saviour's blood and righteousness*
> *My beauty is, my glorious dress;*
> *Thus well arrayed, I need not fear,*
> *When in His presence I appear.*

Beautiful indeed are the lines of Zinzendorf in the following presentation of the Gospel:

> *I thirst, Thou wounded Lamb of God,*
> *To wash me in Thy cleansing blood;*
> *To dwell within Thy wounds; then pain*
> *Is sweet; and life or death is gain.*

So also with John Fletcher, the man who lived closer to God, perchance, than any other man since the days of the apostles:

> *I nothing have, I nothing am,*
> *My treasure's in the bleeding Lamb,*
> *Both now and ever more.*

*

Now the second great experience that came to them was

A Personal Anointing of *the Holy Spirit for Life and Service*

This we have already dealt with. The initial Outpouring was on the whole body of believers at Herrnhut on the morning of August 13th, 1727. In the power of that Anointing they went forth and accomplished impossible tasks.

It only remains to add that all who were gathered to them were taught to likewise receive the Holy Ghost. The experience of the Wesleys and of Whitfield again furnishes a striking illustration. It was during a Moravian Love Feast at Fetter Lane. There were present besides John and Charles Wesley and George Whitfield, five Oxford graduates. But let us hear the story from John Wesley himself.

"About three in the morning, as we were continuing instant in prayer, the power of God came mightily upon us, inasmuch that many cried for exceeding joy, and many fell to the ground. As soon as we were recovered a little from that awe and amazement at the presence of His Majesty, we broke out with one voice, 'We praise Thee, O God; we acknowledge Thee to be the Lord!'"

James Montgomery, the greatest of all Moravian poets, prayed for this anointing in verse:

> *O Spirit of the living God,*
> *In all Thy plenitude of grace,*

> *Where'er the foot of man hath trod,*
>   *Descend on our apostate race.*
> *Give tongues of fire and hearts of love*
>   *To preach the reconciling Word;*
> *Give power and unction from above*
>   *Where'er the joyful sound is heard.*

When John Wesley visited Herrnhut, he heard Christian David, a carpenter, preach four times, who spoke of those who had received forgiveness through the blood of Christ, but who had not received the Anointing of the Holy Ghost.

Again we quote from the pen of James Montgomery:

> *Lord God, the Holy Ghost*
>   *In this accepted hour,*
> *As on the day of Pentecost*
>   *Descend in all Thy power.*

So much for the two outstanding experiences that resulted from the Outpouring on that memorable morning: one, the reception of Christ, and the other, the anointing of the Holy Spirit, separate, definite and vital.

*

Now for the two great results, the fruit produced. And first in order we must mention

Hymns and Spiritual Songs

No church, in comparison to its numbers, has ever

produced as many hymns as the Moravian. For two centuries now we have been singing their hymns. Most of their hymns are prayers to Christ. And many of them are expressions of joy and gratitude for what He has done. In them they portray His sufferings for sinners on the cross. His shed blood is the central theme of their song. Practically all their hymns are hymns of their own personal experiences of salvation and blessing.

Already we have quoted verses from some of these imperishable hymns. It but remains to mention the poets themselves.

Greatest of all among them, and perhaps the outstanding hymn writer of the entire Christian dispensation, was the gifted James Montgomery, a son of John and Mary Montgomery, Moravian missionaries in the West Indies. In most of the great hymnals of the day the following immortal hymns by James Montgomery are to be found: "Angels, from the realms of glory", "Hail to the Lord's Anointed", "Go to dark Gethsemane", "Prayer is the soul's sincere desire", "In the hour of trial", "Forever with the Lord!" etc.

Bishop Gambold's hymn, so loved by Rowland Hill, was:

> And when I'm to die, Receive me, I'll cry,
> For Jesus hath loved me, I cannot tell why.
> But this I do know, we two are so joined,
> He'll not live in glory, and leave me behind.

Another was John Cennick, a great preacher and hymn writer. This from his pen:

We are trav'lling home to God
In the way the fathers trod;
They are happy now and we
Soon their happiness will see.

Lift your eyes ye sons of light,
Zion's city is in sight;
There our endless Home shall be,
There our Lord we soon shall see.

Many, many others there were, far too numerous to mention. But to ignore Charles Wesley, the direct product of Moravianism, would be impossible. Of the hymns he wrote, 6,000 have been published. Hundreds of them are Moravian in their theology. Peter Boehler it was who gave him the thought from which he wrote:

Oh for a thousand tongues to sing
  My great Redeemer's Praise;
The glories of my God and King,
  The triumphs of His grace.

But Wesley's great hymns are far too well known to be quoted here. Yet apart from his conversion through the Moravians and their influence on his life, it is doubtful if one of them could ever have been written.

*

The other outstanding result of the Moravian revival at Herrnhut was

A Vision of World-Wide Missions

"This small church in twenty years," says Dr. Warneck, "called into being more missions than the whole Evangelical Church has done in two centuries."

Even Cowper bore testimony to the spirit of Missions that pervaded the Moravian Church:

> *See Germany send forth*
> *Her sons to pour it on the farthest North;*
> *Fired with a zeal peculiar they defy*
> *The rage and rigour of a polar sky,*
> *And plant successfully sweet Sharon's Rose*
> *On icy plains and in eternal snows.*

That this great missionary fervour was the direct result of the mighty Outpouring at Herrnhut, and that a new and unquenchable passion controlled the entire Movement, is most strikingly set forth by Count Zinzendorf himself:

> *Urged by love, to every nation*
> *Of the fallen human race,*
> *We will publish Christ's salvation,*
> *And declare His blood-bought grace.*

Again their great leader, Count Zinzendorf, imparts to them his vision in the following words:

"I am destined by the Lord to proclaim the

message of the death and blood of Jesus, not with human wisdom but with divine power, unmindful of personal consequences to myself."

But it is in Zinzendorf's last words spoken on his death-bed, that we get the real spirit of Moravianism:

"I am going to my Saviour. I am ready. There is nothing to hinder me now. I cannot say how much I love you all. Who would have believed that the prayer of Christ, 'that they all may be one', could have been so strikingly fulfilled among us! I only asked for the first-fruits among the heathen, and thousands have been given me. Are we not as in Heaven! Do we not live together like angels! The Lord and His servants understand each other. I am ready."

He died at the age of sixty and was buried at Herrnhut, more than four thousand from all parts of the world following his body to the grave.

In the West Indies, among the North American Indians, on the cold, bleak shores of Greenland, far away in dark, benighted Africa, as well as in South America, and practically every country in Europe and Asia, the Moravians planted the Cross and won thousands of souls to Jesus Christ. And all this, let it be remembered, some fifty years before the Modern Missionary Movement was launched by Carey.

Thus as in the days of the Early Church, the Holy Ghost fell upon them, and immediately "they went everywhere preaching the Word" – witnesses unto Christ. And because they were, with Paul, determined to know nothing save Jesus Christ and Him crucified, they were eminently successful. They preached the blood to the most savage tribes, and multitudes were convicted and converted.

It was the spirit expressed in their leader's great motto that inspired them: "I have one passion," exclaimed Zinzendorf, "it is Jesus, Jesus only."

*

But now arises the Question: What about us? Do we need a Revival? What is the greatest need of the Church of our day? Men, machinery, money, organization? No. The supreme need of the hour is a mighty Outpouring of the Holy Ghost. Oh that there might come upon us a spirit of prayer such as came upon the Brethren at Herrnhut two centuries ago, that we, too, both individually and as a Church, might experience an Anointing of the Holy Spirit that would cause the world to wonder at the "signs following!" God grant it may be so!

10

The Greatest Need of the Hour

"And it shall come to pass in the last days, saith God, I will pour out of My Spirit upon all flesh; and your sons and your daughters shall prophesy, and your young men shall see visions, and your old men shall dream dreams: And on My servants and on My handmaidens I will pour out in those days of My Spirit; and they shall prophesy" (Acts 2:17, 18).

Such is God's glorious promise, spoken first of all by the Holy Spirit through the prophet Joel, and again by the same Holy Spirit through the lips of Peter on the day of Pentecost. For ten long days they had waited, a hundred and twenty of them, and now at last Pentecost had come. Oh wonderful hour! With what joyful hearts and radiant faces they could now sing:

The Comforter has come!
The Comforter has come!
The Holy Ghost from Heav'n,
The Father's promise giv'n.
Oh, spread the tidings round
Wherever man is found,
The Comforter has come!

Thank God, He had come! They had not waited in vain. Their Master's promise was at last verified. The Spirit had been poured forth. In obedience they had tarried, no one even suggesting that they commence their great work. They knew that their Lord would be faithful to His Word, and they waited. Now He had come, and they were ready, ready at last to go forth with His glorious Gospel to all the world.

But no sooner had the Holy Ghost come than the crowds began to gather. They did not have long to wait for an audience. Men of every nation and tongue had journeyed to Jerusalem to keep the Feast. Jewish proselytes abounded on every side. And so thousands were soon listening to the new Message. And to the amazement of all, each man was able to hear the Gospel in his own tongue. The disciples were speaking every language and dialect required. "And they were amazed and marvelled, saying one to another, Behold, are not all these which speak Galileans? And how hear we every man in our own tongue, wherein we were born?" And well might their astonishment overwhelm them, for they were listening to simple Galilean fishermen, men who would find it extremely difficult to master any language, suddenly gifted to speak in a foreign tongue, so clearly, so perfectly, mark you, that they needed no interpreter. It was an experience that has never been repeated. (Eph. 4:5. 1 Cor. 12:13).

But they were not all serious. Satan had his emissaries present also. "What meaneth this?" exclaimed the more devout. "Others mocking said, These men are full of new wine."

Now, Peter, to the front and speak. Answer this multitude. You were a coward once, Peter. A little maid scared you. But that was before Pentecost. The Holy Ghost has come upon you, Peter; you can be bold now. Speak, Peter, speak!

But Peter needs no such urging. He is ready in a moment. Oh, no, he has had no time to prepare his sermon. In fact, he wasn't expecting such an audience. But he is ready, nevertheless. He is filled with One who is always ready. And lifting up his great heavy voice, as he stands in the midst of the disciples, he speaks:

"Ye men of Judea, and all ye that dwell at Jerusalem, be this known unto you, and hearken to my words: For these are not drunken, as ye suppose, seeing it is but the third hour of the day. But this is that which was spoken by the prophet Joel."

Never had they heard such a message. Never had they seen such a messenger. Nearer and nearer they crowded, straining to catch every word. Peter had been thinking of Jerusalem only. Now he includes all Israel. His voice rises as he warms to his subject. The Holy Ghost quickens his natural powers, and he continues:

"Ye men of Israel, hear these words; Jesus of Nazareth, a man approved of God among you by miracles and wonders and signs, which God did by Him in the midst of you, as ye yourselves also know: Him, being delivered by the determinate counsel and foreknowledge of God, ye have taken, and by wicked hands have crucified and slain: whom God hath raised up, having loosed the pains of death: because it was not possible that He should be holden of it."

Peter knows no fear as he charges home upon the Jewish nation the murder of God's Son. And with scarcely a pause, he announces still more startling facts:

"This Jesus hath God raised up, whereof we are all witnesses. Therefore being by the right hand of God exalted, and having received of the Father the promise of the Holy Ghost, He hath shed forth this, which ye now see and hear."

Hearts almost cease to beat. Faces turn pale with fear and despair. Anguish is depicted on many a countenance. Sobs and groans are heard spontaneously on every side. The huge multitude sways like a drunken man under the accusation. The Holy Ghost is at work in every heart. The preacher is drawing to a close. His words have fallen like hammer blows, like burning coals of fire, breaking, burning, cutting, piercing in every direction. Suddenly, without a pause, he takes a step forward, and utters his final sentence, as a stillness like death, for a moment, overspreads the entire congregation:

"Therefore let all the house of Israel know assuredly, that God hath made that same Jesus, whom ye have crucified, both Lord and Christ."

The Last Days

"And it shall come to pass in the last days, saith

God, I will pour out of My Spirit upon all flesh."

Now, we are still living in the "last days". This is the dispensation of the Holy Ghost. Pentecost was the birthday of the Church. But if Peter could speak of Pentecost as the "last days", then we are living in the "last hours" of the last days. This is Saturday night in the history of the Church. It is the eleventh hour. Pentecost was the beginning of the "last days". Our generation marks the approaching end of the "last days". The "last hours" are upon us.

God has declared that in the "last days" He would pour out of His Spirit. That promise was partially fulfilled on the day of Pentecost. But it remains for us to see the final and complete fulfilment. Let me again remind you that this is still the dispensation of the Holy Spirit. Have we, then, Scripture to warrant the hope of another great outpouring of the Spirit of God as we enter the "last hours" of the last days of this age? I believe we have. It is my deep, deep conviction that God is waiting to pour out His Spirit once again, and that wherever He can find a people who will meet His conditions, He will give flood-tides of mighty revival. And this, the outpouring of the Holy Spirit, is, I am convinced, the greatest need of the hour.

All may claim a part. It is to be a great universal outpouring for all peoples everywhere. Any one may have it, any church expect it. This is the solution of all problems. Not money, but the outpoured Spirit. Not how to get the attention of the people, but how to secure the operation of the Holy Ghost. Not better preaching, but Holy Ghost preaching. "I will pour out of My Spirit upon all flesh." This, my brethren, is the greatest need of the hour.

Now there was no mistaking what had happened. "This is that" was Peter's verdict. It had been foretold long, long ago. "This is that." Joel had prophesied it, and at last his word had come to pass. "This is that." It was a definite, a genuine, a real experience. Something happened, something so wonderful, so amazing, so unusual that not one could possibly be deluded or deceived. It did not send them in to seek manifestations, it sent them out to do things for God.

How did it happen? What was its cause? Just two things. First, a ten-day prayer meeting. Not a play-meeting, but a prayer meeting. You know we are so busy these days that God cannot get our ear. We will not be quiet and still long enough for Him to speak to us. Prayer, real prayer, hours of unbroken, uninterrupted waiting on God, seems to be largely an experience of the past.

But they waited. God got them still. Do you grasp it? God secured their attention for ten days. Peter forgot his fishing, Matthew his tax collecting. Business was suspended for the time at least. Everything that might detract had been set aside. They "continued with one accord in prayer and supplication". Thus God got them ready. They were now prepared for the mighty outpouring of the Holy Ghost.

And that is still the secret – prayer. Get alone with God. Be quiet long enough for Him to talk. Pray until you are prayed through and prayed out, until you have prayed about every problem. Then when God has settled your problems let Him give you the new vision. Stay in His presence until you can see things through His eyes, until you can see what He wants you to see. He will speak to you about hindrances and obstacles that you never dreamt existed. He will show you what is the matter if you wait long enough. Therefore, don't be impatient at the delay, but pray on and on and on. Delay is not denial. They prayed.

Then they believed God. That is the second condition – faith. They put their trust in His Word. What was that Word? It first occurs in Luke 24:49: "Behold, I send the promise of My Father upon you: but tarry ye in the city of Jerusalem, until ye be endued with power from on high." Then Jesus gave it again in Acts 1:4, 5: "And being assembled together with them, commanded them that they should not depart from Jerusalem, but wait for the promise of the Father, which, saith He, ye have heard of Me. For John truly baptized with water; but ye shall be baptized with the Holy Ghost not many days hence." And finally in Acts 1:8: "But ye shall receive power, after that the Holy Ghost is come upon you: and ye shall be witnesses unto Me both in Jerusalem, and in all Judea, and in Samaria, and unto the uttermost part of the earth."

It was to these promises they pinned their faith. Not to a feeling, nor to a hope, nor a desire, but to the living Word of God. They knew, knew without a doubt, that their Lord's Word would be fulfilled, and they waited.

What Happened?

But what will happen when the Holy Spirit is outpoured? What may we expect? Perhaps if we were to find out what took place as a result of the first great outpouring our question would be answered. What God did once He can do again; and what God did following the outpouring on the day of Pentecost, to a greater or less extent, He will repeat in this our day. Let us see, then, some of the things that followed that mighty outpouring. First of all the disciples were given a supernatural *boldness.* What an amazing difference between the Peter who denied his Lord in the face of a little Jewish maid and the Peter who stood forth like a rock and charged the thousands before him with the murder of the Son of God. Such Holy Ghost boldness is certainly not natural.

In the second place there was supernatural *Power.* That, of course, had been the promise. "Ye shall receive the power of the Holy Ghost." Not a power within themselves imparted by God apart from the all-powerful One, but the power that operated through them from the indwelling Spirit of God. And, oh, the result, the marvellous result of that power! Notice now what happened.

They Were Amazed

"And they were all *amazed*" (Acts 2:12). That was the first thing – amazement. It was written on every face. Men marvelled. "What meaneth this?" The

question was on every tongue. They were astonished, stunned, amazed. What was the explanation?
How account for it? Turn where they would they
listened to the language of their childhood. It was
the most mystifying experience of their lives. And
how the message fastened itself upon their
conscience! What marvellous things they were
hearing! No wonder they were amazed, fascinated.

Ah, my brethren, when has anything happened in
our meeting that has caused amazement? Have
strangers gone out to tell their friends and relatives
of the wonderful works of God? And if not, why
not? Simply because there has been nothing of a
supernatural nature. People are used to the natural.
It is commonplace with them. But have we expected
the supernatural? Is not our religion supernatural?
Then why not look for God to work along supernatural lines?

Yes, and no advertising will be necessary when
the Holy Spirit is outpoured. Nor will there be any
difficulty in getting people to attend the meetings.
Once let something happen that amazes, and there
will be no room for the crowds that will flock to see
what is taking place. People will tell one another
about the amazing things that God is doing, and the
building will be thronged. But it will take the supernatural to do it. "They were amazed." God grant it
in this our day.

They Were Convicted

But not only were they amazed; they were *convicted*.

"Now when they heard this, they were pricked in their heart, and said unto Peter and to the rest of the apostles, Men and brethren, what shall we do?" (Acts 2:37). Ah! the Holy Ghost had been at work. That had been their Lord's promise. "When He (the Holy Ghost) is come, He will convict the world of sin." And so He did. No sooner had He been outpoured upon the disciples than He began to convict the unsaved. And the conviction was real. It made them cry out, "Men and brethren, what shall we do?"

And so it has been and so it ever will be in every genuine outpouring of the Holy Spirit. There will be conviction of sin. Men will be pricked in their heart as on the day of Pentecost. This is the great lack in the work of today. There is little or no conviction. That is what we need today more than anything else – real, old-fashioned conviction that makes people cry out in agony, "What shall we do?"

Strike the stoutest sinner through,
Start the cry, 'What must I do?'
Make him weep till born anew
Through the land.

They Were Converted

Conviction is not conversion. It is possible to be deeply convicted of sin and still never be converted. Unless conviction leads to conversion it has failed in its object. In a real outpouring of the Holy Spirit there are genuine *conversions*.

"Then they that gladly received his word were baptized: and the same day there were added unto them about three thousand souls" (Acts 2:41). "Many of them which heard the word believed; and the number of the men was about five thousand" (Acts 4:4). "And believers were the more added to the Lord, multitudes both of men and women" (Acts 5:14).

So not only was there Holy Ghost boldness and Holy Ghost power and Holy Ghost conviction, but also Holy Ghost conversions. People were saved. They had passed from death unto life. Apart from the salvation of souls the Church has no ground for her existence. We are saved to win others. And when the Holy Spirit is outpoured souls will be definitely, eternally saved.

They Came Gladly

"Then they that *gladly* received his word were baptized" (Acts 2:41). That was the way they were saved – gladly. It wasn't necessary to coax and urge, to plead and entreat. They came, and came gladly. Their danger was real and they saw it. "Escape for thy life" was the spirit in which they acted. "Men and brethren, what shall we do?" became the cry on every side.

But, oh, my brethren, how different it is today! How we stand and plead! Sometimes for twenty minutes the evangelist will urge sinners to be saved. And then at last, after resisting for all that time, someone will finally step out into the aisle, and slowly, with head up, walk forward to the inquiry room, as though doing God an honour.

But was it so on the day of Pentecost? No, indeed. They were anxious, they were glad to come. Conviction was real. The message had gone home. The Spirit had done His work. There was a great load on their backs of which they had suddenly become conscious, and to get it off was now their one and only thought.

They Continued Steadfastly

"And they *continued steadfastly*" (Acts 2:42). That is to say, they did not backslide. The real reason there are so many backsliders is because there are so many who have never had a true forward slide to Jesus Christ. Their conversion has been that of the head instead of the heart. They have never possessed what they professed. They have come forward and committed themselves to Christ, but they have never been saved, they have never been converted, they have not been born again.

Charles G. Finney was probably the greatest revivalist since the days of the Apostles. His sermons were largely on sin and its consequences. He appealed to the conscience through the Word of God. Hence, his converts stood. Only fifteen per cent, we are told, ever backslid. Whereas, with even so great a preacher as D. L. Moody, quite a large number, it is reported, went back. And in Wesley's work, including all the holiness groups that have sprung from it, though one of the mightiest of all-time, the one great cry of anguish has been over the vast army of backsliders.

But it was not so in the Early Church. The Word says, "They continued steadfastly". Surely, then, there is room for deep searchings of heart as to the cause of so much backsliding. Surely it behoves us to ask God to test our work and see what it produces. Ought we not to be able to come back five, yea, ten years after, and find our converts standing true?

A backslider is a curse. Nothing so pains the body and head as a dislocated member. A dislocation does not mean a separation. I am speaking now of the true backslider, one who has really been born again. The arm may be dislocated and yet not severed. But, oh, the pain, not only to it, but to the whole body, and also to the head! So with the backslider.

They Praised God

There is still another characteristic that cannot be overlooked. In Acts 2:47 it says of them that they were *"praising God"*. Ah, yes! when there is real birth there is a cry. The first thing a newborn babe in Christ does is to say: "Abba, Father." It somehow comes natural. It springs spontaneously from the heart. And so they praised the Lord. They praised Him daily. Praise was the natural expression of their new-found joy.

But so many of our converts seem to be "still-born". And when they are asked to testify they have to be coaxed and urged. Then they get up and repeat a short verse of Scripture.

But, oh, when the Holy Spirit is outpoured – how different! Why, they can hardly be kept still. They all want to testify at once. Their hearts are full and overflowing. Nor can they praise Him enough for all He has done.

They Were Persecuted

"All that will live godly in Christ Jesus shall suffer *persecution*" (2 Tim. 3:12). So it ever has been and so it ever will be. No sooner had the Holy Spirit been poured out than the Devil began to rage. Almost immediately they were brought into conflict with the priests and Sadducees. And the next thing they knew they were behind the bars.

Don't ever dream that the priests and Sadducees are all dead. Not by a long way. And when the Holy Ghost is poured out they will be the very first to oppose. Persecution always comes from the religious people, and generally from the leaders themselves. Every Spirit-filled man has found it so.

The Russian believers were persecuted by the Greek Orthodox Church, and martyred by hundreds, or sent into Siberian exile. The Lutheran Church of Sweden became the terrible agency for the torture of the Christians in that country. John Wesley suffered most of all from the clergy and laity of the Established Church of England.

Now what actually happened? They were questioned of course. And, oh, the answers that Peter gave! What Holy Ghost boldness! What fearlessness! And finally, since there was nothing else to do, they let them go, first commanding them never again to speak or teach in the name of Jesus.

Well, did they agree to the terms? Did they obey? Not for a moment. "Whether it be right in the sight of God," replied Peter, "to hearken unto you more than unto God, judge ye. For we cannot but speak the things which we have seen and heard." Hallelujah! "So when they had further threatened them, they let them go, finding nothing how they might punish them" (Acts 4:19-21).

Now what is to be the plan of procedure? What would Worldly Wiseman counsel? I think I can hear him even now. "Be cautious," he advises. "Keep quiet. Obey the rulers and don't preach any more for a while. Wait till the storm blows over. Bow to authority and so escape further trouble."

But do they listen to Worldly Wiseman? Not for a moment. No sooner are they free than they hurry to their own company and report everything. Then they hold a great rousing prayer-meeting. "And now, Lord, behold their threatenings": they exclaim, "and grant unto Thy servants, that with all boldness they may speak Thy Word" (Acts 4:23–30).

Think of it – asking for greater boldness than ever! Yes, and God gloriously answers their prayer (Acts 5:12–16). And then – well, then it happened just as Worldly Wiseman had predicted. They found themselves in jail again (Acts 4:17–42). And, oh, what an experience! Once again they were reprimanded and warned, after which they were given a beating, and then let go.

And how did they take it? Did they console one

another and say: "Oh, Andrew, didn't it hurt?" "Yes, Peter, it was simply awful." 'And think of it," adds John, "we have been in jail twice already within the past few days. How will we ever show our faces again?" "I think it is too much altogether," declares Andrew, "we have had enough."

Did they talk like that? Well, I should say not. Listen, this is what happened: "And they departed from the presence of the Council, rejoicing that they were counted worthy to suffer shame for His name."

Oh, my brethren, I sometimes wish there were a little more persecution in the Church today. The line of demarcation would be clearly drawn then. Mere professors would soon fall away, while God's true children would suffer and go through. It would do us good. But this I know, let revival come and persecution will accompany it. It always follows the outpouring of the Holy Spirit.

They Prayed

The next thing I notice is that there was poured upon them a wonderful spirit of *prayer*. What a prayer-meeting they had following the first release from prison! (Acts 4:23–31). How important they considered it! "We will give ourselves continually to prayer and the ministry of the Word," they vowed. And on the night of Peter's deliverance from prison – oh, how they prayed! No time for sleep. Too much was at stake. And prayer, continuous, fervent, united intercession, could alone prevail. So they prayed, prayed until their prayers were answered.

My friends, prayer has been the outcome as well as the secret of every mighty outpouring all down the centuries. Oh, the spirit of prayer that rested on the converts of the revival under Finney! And the early Methodists – oh, how they prayed! What a spirit of intercession possessed them! How fervently they pled with God! Think of William Bramwell spending thirty-six hours in fasting and prayer.

And when the Holy Ghost is again poured out there will fall upon the people a spirit of prayer. Prayer is the natural atmosphere of every true revival. Would to God we had more of it!

The Holy Ghost Fell Upon Them

One of the most striking examples of the outpouring of the Holy Spirit is found in the incident of the household of Cornelius. Peter in describing the experience says, "As I began to speak the Holy Ghost fell upon them" (Acts 11:15). Has there ever been a time in our experience when we could give such a report?

Something definite, something unusual, something extraordinary must have taken place. And it is this that we need today more than anything else in the world. It is unquestionably the greatest need of the hour. God can do more in five minutes when the Holy Ghost is poured out than we can accomplish in a lifetime apart from such a divine intervention.

It is possible, I say again, to hold great evangelistic campaigns, to report hundreds of conversions, to have much enthusiasm, large crowds, wonderful sermons, splendid newspaper accounts, excellent singing, good music, and everything else that pleases the natural mind and satisfies the worldly Christian. But of what use are these if, after the evangelist goes and the campaign is over, the prayer meetings are no larger than before, the converts, so-called, quickly return to the life they have always lived, the church settles down to its usual formality and coldness, and the great revival(?) becomes almost extinct? Why is such the case? Simply because the one thing needful was lacking. The report of Peter, "As I began to speak the Holy Ghost fell upon them," could never once be said of the meetings held.

Wesley

When Wesley finished his message he closed his eyes and called upon God to confirm His Word, to bear witness to His truth, and to set His seal, and God did. He was immediately vindicated. Men and women dropped on every side under deep conviction of sin, and with loud cries besought God to have mercy upon them. Thus the bystanders knew that John Wesley was God's servant of a truth, that his message was divine, and that the Holy Spirit was present in mighty power; for no sooner had the great preacher concluded his sermon and called upon God than the Holy Ghost was poured out upon the people, resulting in the conviction and conversion of sinners.

Finney

It was so in the ministry of Charles G. Finney. A few words spoken in the power of the Spirit made a lasting and a saving impression upon scores. In fact, everyone to whom he spoke during the first day following his remarkable anointing with the Spirit, was sooner or later converted. Wherever he preached there was deep conviction. Again and again, as he proclaimed the Message, the Holy Spirit was suddenly poured out upon the people, so that large numbers were swept into the Kingdom.

He was one day preaching in a schoolhouse. At first the people became angry, then suddenly everything changed. The Holy Spirit fell, and in a moment every person in the audience was on his knees crying aloud for mercy. So great were the groans and cries of anguish that for some time the evangelist was unable to make himself heard as he attempted to point the stricken ones to Christ. For Finney this was a common experience. He always preached with the expectation of seeing the Holy Spirit suddenly outpoured. Until this happened little or nothing was accomplished. But the moment the Spirit fell upon the people, Finney had nothing else to do but point them to the Lamb of God. Thus he lived and wrought for years in an atmosphere of revival.

Brainerd

David Brainerd had the same experience. For months he had laboured among the Indians with but little apparent effect. But, suddenly, one day while he was speaking, as in the case of Peter, the Holy Ghost fell upon the Indians, and in a moment they dropped to the ground and began to cry for mercy. Some continued in agony for hours before they were enabled to believe God and venture their all on the atoning blood. Thus at one meeting David Brainerd saw more accomplished than during all the months of his previous labours. How truthfully he could write in reporting what had taken place, "As I began to speak the Holy Ghost fell upon them."

Moody

The unique ministry of D. L. Moody was no exception. He, too, saw the Spirit outpoured. It was when he had crossed the Atlantic to England. The morning service was cold and powerless and Moody closed it without any special sense of God's presence.

In the evening, however, all was different. As he began to speak he noticed a remarkable change in the atmosphere, so much so that at the close of his message he felt constrained to give an invitation. To his amazement almost the entire audience consisting of some four hundred people arose simultaneously. Much mystified he asked them to be seated and then again gave the invitation, this time making it much clearer. Once more the entire audience stood. Again he asked them to sit down. Turning to the minister he sought for an explanation but the minister himself was more than dumbfounded. Presently he turned again to the people, telling them that he wanted none except those who had never been saved. Then, asking all who desired salvation to enter an adjoining room, he closed the service. But when he reached the room indicated he found it packed to capacity.

God had come. The Holy Ghost had been poured out. Hundreds had suddenly been brought under conviction and swept into the Kingdom. How glorious to see God work! What great things are accomplished when the Spirit falls upon the people!

Oh, what a challenge! What a glorious experience! Are we going to expect it? Do we really believe that we are living in the last hours of the last days of this age, and that God's promise is going to be fulfilled? Let us listen to it once again: "And it shall come to pass in the last days, saith God, I will pour out of My Spirit upon all flesh."

May God make it real in our ministry and grant us again and again a mighty outpouring of the Holy Spirit! May we seek Him fervently through prayer and supplication for this, the greatest need of the hour!

RHP One Pound Classics

DAVID WILKERSON
Hungry For More of Jesus
The way of intimacy with Christ
Hallowed Be Thy Names
Knowing God as you've never known Him before

ANDREW MURRAY
The True Vine
Fruitfulness and stability in Jesus

ROY HESSION
The Power of God's Grace
The way of peace, joy and genuine revival
We Would See Jesus
Finding in Jesus everything we need

OSWALD J SMITH
The Revival We Need
A heart-stirring cry for revival
The Enduement of Power
The power of the Holy Spirit in the Christian life

CHARLES FINNEY
Revival
God's way of revival

Please ask for these titles at your
local Christian bookshop

RHP One Pound Classics

The True Vine

by Andrew Murray

A fruitful Christian life is available to every believer, and all that is necessary is to abide in Christ. In this classic devotional, Andrew Murray leads us there.

"When Jesus says, 'I am the true Vine,' He tells us that all the vines of earth are pictures and emblems of Himself. He is the divine reality, of which they are the created expression. They all point to Him, and reveal Him. If you would know Jesus, study the vine.

"How many eyes have gazed on and admired a great vine with its beautiful fruit. Come and gaze on the heavenly Vine till your eye turns from all else to admire Him. How many, in a sunny clime, sit and rest under the shadow of a vine. Come and be still under the shadow of the true Vine, and rest under it from the heat of the day. What countless numbers rejoice in the fruit of the vine! Come, and take, and eat of the heavenly fruit of the true Vine, and let your soul say: 'I sat under His shadow with great delight, and His fruit was sweet to my taste.'"

— ANDREW MURRAY

Now available from your local Christian bookshop